Co
Abilities

Authors:

Baker Jacinto
&
Deidra Rae

CONSCIOUS ABILITIES
Copyright © 2020 Baker Jacinto & Deidra Rae

Disclaimer: Each story and technique described in this book is based on real-life personal experiences that the authors have worked with directly and that have helped them personally. The authors do not claim to be trained professional medical doctors. The authors of this book are not responsible for any medical related, or health related issues that you may have. If you are having any conditions that require serious medical attention consult your physician directly.

Front cover image by Deidra Rae
ISBN: 9798648731974

Conscious Abilities
Table of Contents

Foreword: Dear Human (Deidra Rae)................5
Section One:
    1. How Being the Authentic Self
       Leads to A Better World....................6
    2. Managing the Chaos.........................14
    3. The Mind...................................19
    4. The Heart..................................27
    5. The Body - Living Authentically...........34
    6. Consciously Directing Your Life...........45
    7. Living Authentically
       Using the Tools You Have..................52
    8. The Flow State and Receiving Signs.......62
    9. Thriving with Passion......................69
    10. We Are One................................76
    11. Humanity and Singularity..................86
    12. Utopia....................................94

Section Two: 105

   13. How Language Shapes Your Reality...........110

   14. Empathy 101................................117

   15. Jesus Christ...............................125

   16. Intuition.................................131

   17. Visions...................................138

   18. This Message Is Brought to You By...???....147

   19. Fate v Destiny............................152

   20. Ego.......................................158

   21. The Beginning of a New Era.................170

   22. Dear Human (Baker).........................176

Authors' Biography:...........................177

Baker Jacinto....................................177

Deidra Rae.......................................177

Foreword:

Dear Human,

For whatever reason, you have been drawn to this book. There is something inside you that tells you there is more to what we have been taught to believe. You look at the world around you and you *know*... something has to change.

What we (the authors) have written here is nothing new, the applications may be new to you. We are not doctors or scientists. We are two humans who have been studying and piecing together the mysteries of life, our whole lives. What we have done is simply explained what scientists have discovered about the atom, energy, and consciousness. These discoveries are mainstream. We also give you the motivational means to practice these applications in your life.

We are providing you with a guide, while you choose how you navigate your life path. This is the book we wish was available when we were beginning to figure it all out. We only had to wait for science to catch up with what the ancients knew

Books are guides, to help you unlock your knowledge within. Discard what does not resonate with your soul. Remember who you are and why you are here.

With love,
Deidra Rae

Chapter 1: How Being the Authentic Self Leads to A Better World

"I think, therefore I am." (Descartes, 1637) You probably have heard this quote before, and maybe Descartes was on to something; that moment Consciousness is aware of Free Will. What if actually being the Authentic Self was connected to everything else in the world? Mainly, being the authentic self was indeed connected directly to making the world a better place... You see, we live in a world where we experience so much contrast. People with so many different views, whether it be religious, political, race, sexual orientation, etc. The list goes on and on. But, what if for once there was something, we can do to really bridge the gap? Put all our differences aside, and for once come back to being something so powerful, so special, so grand, that in coming back to this one thing. It literally changes the world.

Imagine going back to the essence of it all. Going back to the simple things in life, going back to something so simple yet so powerful, that indeed this simple switch brings us back to the all-powerful authentic self. The same authentic self that brings about a change in the world. A utopia so to speak, that begins with, well us.

A solid foundation for where we can begin to attempt to make this world a better place would definitely start with our own personal values. Imagine a world where every human's values were aligned for the highest and best good of all of humanity.

Imagine if every human on planet earth practiced good values. If every human did this, it would make sense that we can all come to some sort of starting point, an ideal standard of living, where we can all coexist in this beautiful utopia here on earth. The real question then remains...

Are "good values" more important than love, happiness, and your feelings? First, it is impossible to have good values without some sense of love and happiness, and it is impossible to ignore your feelings when considering what are good values. What one person may consider being of good value, or morally good, may be contradictory to another person's idea of what is good; perspective is subjective.

Secondly, what you feel is part of (not limited to) love and happiness. The concepts are not separate from one another, but rather it is the same thing. Our verbal language often limits us from describing what we feel. So, to say, "I feel like doing..." That is not an emotion; that is a physical extension of that emotion with a thought attachment and quite often a subjective desire to fill an emotional void. The "good values" we hold on to are there to guide us to find what is most important.

Having good values is important but can cause a battle of emotions within you. Does this mean you should ignore the values and go with what you feel? No. Does this mean you have to sacrifice your own happiness to hold on to good values? No. Does this mean you have to be nice and kind to people when internally you feel like giving them a piece of your mind or more? No, but if you feel like the latter over choosing kindness, then there is a deeper issue within you that you still need to resolve.

Good values and morals are there to guide us. Guide us to what? There is something deeper, more important than anything else; something that everything else is merely an extension of. You could say it is love, but love is only one piece of the equation. You could say it is happiness, but that is only an extension of love. You could say it is what you feel (still another emotion with physical attachment). Are you scratching your head, yet? Imagine this scenario:

Mind: Why are we awake? [consciously thinking]
Heart: We have a world to explore. [loving life]
Body: Wake up you two. Let us combine our powers and work as one. [spreading the love]

The Authentic Self

To give it a label, we will call it "The Authentic Self" to give you an understanding of what we are attempting to describe here. It is a trinity that makes up the core of your being; thought, heart, and action -or- your mind, your spirit, and your physical body. Ancient symbols have been used to describe the relation for this trinity, such as the triskelion, triquetra, and the trinity knot. Three important pieces that work together.

Thought (mind) — The mind has extraordinary abilities. It works consciously and subconsciously. We use our thoughts to learn new things, to remember the past, to make decisions for the future, to move through the present, and when we dream, the mind reveals our deeper thoughts. When we consider our values, we use thought to guide us. Our emotions can have a direct effect on the thoughts we have, however, we do have the ability to override what we feel and use our thought to redirect our choices.

Spirit (heart) — There are only two true emotions: love and fear; all other emotions extend from these two. Happiness, joy, excitement, content, etc are extensions of love. Anger, hatred, frustration, worry, etc are extensions of fear. We are born with love; fear is learned. Humans are naturally compassionate. It is when we are introduced to our current world stimuli, we learn to judge and begin to fear what we do not understand. The more we fear, the further away we get from being who we truly are. Our natural state of being is love and that love is expressed into the physical world through happiness, peacefulness, kindness, and compassion. With this, to find your way back to the core of your being, you must find the love within you.

Action (body) — The physical body is the vehicle we use to move through our lives. Some of our actions are voluntary, some are involuntary. Our conscious thoughts become a physical action when we make a decision.

Our emotions are expressed physically through actions. For instance, a tantrum is a physical response to anger and laughter is a physical response to joy. Without the physical body, the energy created by our mind and heart would simply drift around the universe.

The True Authentic Self

Here is the most interesting part. The trinity between the three (mind-heart-body) is the makeup of your being. If any one of these pieces of the trinity is missing or does not match the other two, you are not being true to yourself. When these three work together in harmony, you are being authentic. When you match your thoughts, emotions, and actions, you will have connected to the core of your being, the authentic self.

Balancing the Authentic Self

Now, if you are thinking of harming someone, your emotions are full of hate (extension of fear), and you take action to cause harm, this is not being the true self. Yes, we did say all three work together, but if the emotion is an extension of fear you are expressing a learned behavior and have distanced yourself from who you really are. Most likely, that behavior is your own ego filling a void and has created an alternate form of fear in an attempt to justify what you feel.

If you feel like eating junk food, you take the action to do so. On the other hand, somewhere within you, those good values are guiding what you are doing is not healthy for you. If you eat junk food anyway, ignoring 1/3 of the self, you are not being the true you.

If you show kindness to someone because those good values guided you to do so, but you feel some bitterness towards the person you are being kind to and your thoughts are wishing you chose to do something else, you are not being the true you. If you are battling your feelings, are you really listening to your heart? You have somehow chosen to focus on a negative perspective and follow the learned behavior driven by fear.

Almost everything that is wrong with the world is that people are driven by a fear of what they do not understand with an ego desire to have control. What is wrong is people pretend to be something they are not, ignoring what they feel, and thinking about what they really want or worried about what they do not want. They have forgotten who they really are; a being born of love, who is meant to use the mind (both logically and creatively) and take action with passion.

It is not wrong to feel anger or fear for the short-term. These emotions are motivators, to protect what you love. Fear, and extensions of fear, are your gauge to understand just how deep you feel. To put it simply, how would you know when you are happy if you are never sad? How would you know what love is if you never felt heartbreak?

For the long-term, find your way back to that authentic state of mind, your center where you are clear-minded and driven with passion. Moderation is also key. It is perfectly fine to enjoy the little things, remember to experience and live life.

If you are missing any one of the three variables of the authentic self-trinity, you will be off-balance and your life, mentality, and health become chaos. You must align all three pieces of the equation to find the balance. Your life may be divided up into different parts, but the one thing each part has in common is you. Be a powerful force by being the true you in all aspects of your life.

When you make the choice to use your mind to focus on positive perspectives, using good values as a guide, to direct your emotions to the various extensions of love, and take actions that match what you think and feel, you will not only find yourself in a much more peaceful state of being, you will be driven by a passion that becomes an unstoppable force. You will discover a world that will open up for you in magical ways. Can you imagine what the world would be like if everyone found and lived authentically, a life with love, kindness, and compassion? We know it is a long shot, but certainly not impossible. It begins with You.

May you find the information in this book helpful. Like many others, we grew up in a world being told that these abilities are not real or evil. Science is catching up to what the ancients knew. It is real and the only way it could be evil would be through the intention of what you do with it.

Before you dismiss this concept of human mind / Conscious Abilities, remember You Have Free Will. Are you certain what you have been taught to believe is true? Or are you open to the possibilities and ready to grow, expand your mind and learn more? Keep reading.

Chapter 2: Managing the Chaos

Every day, humans are faced with challenges, experiences, and emotional lessons. These challenges usually come in the form of chaos. Chaos in the external environment; the physical, and also chaos that comes from within one's own inner world; the mind and heart. *One of the best things you can do is MASTER the chaos in you. You are not thrown into the fire; YOU ARE THE FIRE.* A Consciousness aware of Free Will, allowing you to choose what you believe, the attitude you have, and how you respond to chaos.

Everything is made up of energy. Many spiritual belief systems believe that there is a life force, a soul, the center of our being. Science began to catch up. Quantum Physics proves that solid matter does not exist. Everything is made up of atoms. Atoms are energy. Therefore, everything is energy, including your thoughts. Brain waves can be measured. Your thoughts are energy. The heart's magnetic field can be measured outside of the body. And with the mass of your physical body (atoms), You are energy. Your thought begins it, your emotion amplifies it, and your action increases the momentum.

If your entire make-up is energy? Would you need to ground that energy, especially if you want to consciously manage and direct it? Grounding yourself is important. You may have heard the term before. But what does it mean?

Grounding

In electrical terms is connecting the electrical current to the ground, to prevent shock. For a human, grounding is connected to the earth, being in the moment. You're probably thinking, "Pssh, I've never grounded myself. And I'm fine." You most likely have many times over your life and did not realize it.

How does consciously grounding oneself help? Grounding can clear your mind. Recharge your energy. Calm your emotions. Giving you better abilities to focus and direct your life. How do you know if you are UNgrounded? Do you feel scattered, airy, just a little off?

There are many ways to ground yourself. Go for a walk barefoot in the grass, visualizing rooting to the ground. Remember you are not physically rooting to the ground; you can still move. This is a conscious visualization. Seriously, imagine tree roots growing out of you and into the earth. Getting out into nature is the best way to ground and connect to the earth; this method is not always a viable option for everyone. There are other ways to consciously ground yourself: You can root yourself indoors and on the top floor (long roots), potting plants (getting your hands in soil), and physical exercise are other methods. There are many ways for a person to consciously ground themselves.

The best part is, unlike electrical currents, you do not need to stay physically connected to the earth to be grounded. It is the conscious awareness you are awakening by the physical and conscious act. So, go hug a tree!... Inhale through your nose and exhale through your mouth; taking long deep breaths. Much like what you would do in meditation. You can do this with your eyes open or closed, whichever way you are comfortable.

Meditation

The purpose of meditation is to train your attention and awareness and achieve a mentally clear and emotionally calm and stable state. How does one meditate?

"The Power of the Breath As you sit here and read this, you are breathing, from moment to moment without even paying attention to it. The body breathes automatically. The breath, the inhalation, and exhalation of air is a wonderful tool you carry with you everywhere you go. You can use it to come back to the present moment and find your center again. Here is a meditation technique used in the mindfulness practice. Find a quiet place and sit comfortably and as erect as you can, like a helium balloon is attached to the crown of your head and gently pulling you up to help you to keep your spine straightened. Close your eyes and sit comfortably. Take a moment to arrive in the here and now.

Check-in with yourself and what is going on within you. Be gentle to yourself. Bring your attention to the physical sensation of your body, and just notice. I suggest you move your attention from one to the next body part after about two breaths. Starting at your head, your face, your neck, throat, shoulders and arms, chest, back and belly pelvis and legs, feet. Notice any sensation without judgment. You may decide to release some of the tension by gently breathing into the tense areas. As best as you can, bring your attention to the sensation of breathing.

Take a moment to just observe your breath. Feel as the air enters your nostrils, how your chest and then your belly rises as you inhale and how the belly and chest fall again as you exhale. Let go of controlling your breath, just let the breath happen by itself, the body knows how to breathe. Watch it, how it happens from moment to moment, with spacious awareness, meaning be a witness without trying to change or control it.

"The breath is your present moment anchor point. Soon your mind will start to wander, but do not worry, that is part of the exercise process. As you notice, your mind is thinking, you just gently let go, jump off that train of thought and bring your attention back to your breath as best as you can. You are training the mind, which is like a muscle. Over time, you will get better. Do not judge yourself about thinking too much or not doing it right, this meditation practice is like a cycle. Just be, accept where you are right now is where you are supposed to be in your practice. You may sit as long as you feel comfortable with this practice, you may use a timer. I started with five minutes a day. Some people prefer to do some deep breathing which is great too.

Another Breathing Exercise You may choose to visualize the air you breathe in as clear and light filled. As it enters your body you feel it wash through you and as you exhale you visualize the air exiting as a dark cloud, having cleared out any negativity."
(Simone Blaise)

Centering

It is important to balance the mind and feelings (your emotions). No, it is not a physical thing where you stand straight with your arms out, touching your nose to your face, and get yourself balanced. Centering is a mental/emotional thing... to understand it, here is a visualization / meditation technique:

Think of your thoughts and emotions like a hurricane. All your thoughts and the feelings attached to those thoughts are swirling around. It can be destructive internally and externally without some management. At the center of the hurricane, that is you, YOUR center; the eye of the storm, where you are calm / clear, and you have management of the direction. Visualize yourself as the hurricane, and sense your energy surrounding you. Pull it all into your center, where you have calmed the chaos, and the ability to choose which direction to focus.

When your inner voice sounds clearer to you than the voice of the outside world, you find inner peace. By consciously grounding and centering your thoughts and emotions, you are aligning your intentions. Allowing yourself to choose and manage your direction.

Chapter 3: The Mind

The Thoughts We Have Carry Power. — The thoughts we think on a regular basis carry power. The thoughts we think and carry in our mind have power and how we decide to think about any circumstance in our life is what we are actually creating in our life.

Every thought, with the emotion attached to that thought, shapes your perspective. The attitude you hold toward a circumstance or belief, becomes a magnetic force of energy, creating and attracting your experiences. Many ancient texts and teachings provided the instructions and clues:

"As a man thinks, so is he." (Proverbs 23:7)

"Whatever you say or do, good or bad, will eventually return to you." (Karma)

"All that we are is the result of what we have thought." (Buddha)

"Man prays for evil, as he prays for good; man is ever hasty." (Quran 17:11)

"Do unto others as you would have them do unto you." (Golden Rule)

"Let him who would move the world first move himself." (Socrates)

"...the power of the world always works in circles, and everything tries to be round." (Black Elk - Oglala Lakota)

"A man is but the product of his thoughts - what he thinks, he becomes." (Mahatma Gandhi)

In the 1990s, Japanese alternative medicine doctor Masaru Emoto did a few experiments observing the actual material physical effect words, music, and prayers had on crystalline water. His studies scientifically found that depending on the actual nature words and thoughts that were directed towards the water under a microscope the structure of the water would change form. For example, when the water is frozen its crystals will be depicted as "beautiful" or "ugly" depending on whether the words and thoughts were positive or negative. As subjective as this may be...

So, a Man did an experiment to study the effects of words and the attitude attached to the words have on crystallized water. Before you roll your eyes, consider how you would react to this experiment if it had been done by a 14-year-old, who had won a science award for the experiment. We already know our emotions have a physical effect on our health and well-being. The thoughts we choose to tell ourselves have a direct effect on our attitude and perspective. Imagine what happens with the words and thoughts we think daily in our own minds since our human bodies are on an average of 60% water.

It goes without saying, your attitude and your perspective will shape your experiences. The words you choose have an energetic impact. You are literally, creating your life with the thoughts that dominate your mind, coupled with your attitude. You are the observer and author of your story. Every story you are repeating in your head either silently, or out loud in conversation with others carries an energy that actually is creating your future.

The Observer Effect

The popular quantum physics double-slit experiment to put it simply. Energy particles were sent through two separate slits and formed a distinct pattern on the wall beyond the two slits. The patterns showed that the energy particles had vibrational waves and influenced the behavior of the individual particles. Then they attempted to observe how energy particles influenced the behavior.

What the scientists discovered is when a vibrational wave interferes with another vibrational wave, the direction of the vibrational wave shifts. To give you a visual, it is like dropping a rock into a pool of water. The water ripples in waves outward. But if you drop a second rock in close proximity to the first set of ripples, the ripples of the second rock will change the behavior of the water ripples of both the first rock and the second rock.

The results of a quantum mechanics double-slit experiment showed that the very act of observing the behavior of energy particles, interfered with the behavior of the particles, thus changing the behavior. So, if particles are influenced by a conscious observer or a thought, that would mean: Thoughts are also energy with vibrational waves.

Energy exists everywhere. Where you focus your attention, shaped by your beliefs, the energy collapses into an observable particle(s). Your awareness and perspective creates the reality you observe.

To be good at manifesting more of what you want in life, versus what you do not want, you have to understand that each person is living and manifesting their reality by the stories they tell themselves via their subconscious mind. Some stories interact with others, but the one thing you cannot do is override another person's, Free Will. If you change the story, you actually start to change the outcome of your manifestations, and therefore the outcomes of your life.

If you ever see people making the same mistakes in life and are frustrated and complaining about their lifetime and time again, then you will find someone that is repeating the same thoughts and energy patterns within themselves and someone is going in circles and never really growing in their life.

Then you see people who are thriving, growing, and always getting better results in life because they are constantly changing their negative situations into positive situations, because of the story they are choosing to tell. They are choosing to avoid a negative perspective and tell the story with a positive attitude.

They are hopeful, and more optimistic in their approach towards problems they face, because they know that it's the story, they are saying either silently in their heads, or out loud in conversation with others that are indeed creating their future.

Wait a minute… You are probably thinking, "There is no way I created this life." Think back. Do you see any patterns in your life? Relationship patterns? Lifestyle? Geographical location? Or even a pattern with the people you associate with? Those patterns were created by the story you keep telling yourself. The lessons keep repeating until you learn and change the way you are thinking; The good news is you are consciously aware of this ability, your Free Will gives you the power to choose your perspective and your attitude, recreating and influencing a different thought energy pattern. Life will manifest for you in physical reality to the proportion of what you are vibrating at energetically.

The Story You Are Telling Now Creates Your Future

Your past is a part of who you are, but it does not define who you will become. Take your experiences, learn from your mistakes, and be the author and master of your story. Every day is a brand-new day that allows you a chance to grow. True growth only happens when we acknowledge our past failures and look to improve upon them. So, although you may have had a past filled with mistakes and failures. It is important to change your story from something that may be holding you back, into a story that empowers and encourages you to keep going forward in your life.

An example would be let's say you failed to get into the college you really wanted to attend all your life. No matter how hard you tried, you ended up in the college you did not want to attend. At that moment, you may feel like you are a failure. The story is, you tried your best to get into the college you always wanted to go, you studied hard, you did more than the other students in a class, and you did whatever it took to get to that college you always wanted to attend, but you were not accepted.

What if that story you tell, can be shifted into a more positive story that actually empowers you? What is the positive story you can tell yourself that encourages you in a more positive way?

The NEW story you can tell yourself is: "Well, I didn't get into the college I wanted, but at least I get to go to college in the first place. I know I tried my best, but this college is closer to my home, so the commute won't be so bad, and well I know there are some new people I am going to meet."

Simply, by looking at the perceived failure, and adding more positive elements (adding positive stories) to it can make a world of difference to your new perspective. Gratitude is the key. Simply, by being thankful for the experience, focusing on the positive details; gives you the *conscious ability* to change the pattern. By telling your story from a more positive perspective, you are also changing the low vibe pattern of your attitude towards that particular situation to something closer to love, bringing you back to your authentic self.

The story you tell yourself, especially about your past is what you recreate in your life in your present and your future. So be careful of the story you tell others. For your story creates your future; silently or spoken aloud.

The good news, however, is that you can create a new story if you choose to create a new story. One idea is to write in a journal the story of how you would like your day or life to unfold. Even in journaling what you put out whether it was true or not actually ends up becoming true for you in the future.

Positive affirmations are some people's choice of living life with a good attitude; or if you prefer a more subtle approach, silently in your head speak kindly to yourself and imagine how you would like your story to develop.

It does not matter what people think about it, or how others perceive it, you are actually the author of how the story goes. So, because you have Free Will, your own conscious mind has the ability to override any previous thoughts, you have the conscious ability to choose your attitude and your perspective. Because you are the author of how the story goes, that means you are creating the past in your favour if you choose to make it a better story for you in the future. The reality is that we are constantly telling stories anyway.

Let us explore a quite simple example. One that is used in typical everyday conversations you have with people. When you spark a conversation with a friend or someone on the street. The question is almost always, "How are you?" Your response is "I am doing good." Or you may respond with "I am not doing so well today." Then you complete that statement with a story or event of what just recently happened in your life. It can be a big story or a small story. It can be a negative or positive story. Nevertheless, it is a story. It is a story that you are creating. It may be an actual story of describing what actually happened, or maybe not as exact of how it happened, but nevertheless, it is a story that you are sharing from your perspective.

That story that you are sharing is shaping your reality because the thoughts we think most of the time become things and what we say on a regular basis (out loud in conversation or thoughts kept silently) is what is adding to the energy moment of what is creating our future.

Now, there are actual events that took place in that story that has recently happened to you as you share the story. However, how you decide to tell it with what emotions you leave out or put in creating your future.

So, remember we live life, we experience things and events. How we perceive those things and events is our story. The attitude you attach to your story becomes the fuel, the motivator to move your conscious thought energy.

What story are you telling? Energy cannot be destroyed. It is only shifted and transformed. Every thought you have creates the reality you are personally experiencing.

Are you mad? That moment you realize you have the conscious ability to create a better life for yourself. But hold on… "If all I have to do is imagine my dream world, why is the world so messed up?"

Remember, everyone has Free Will, and every human is creating what they perceive as their version of the world. That is a lot of energy particles interacting and influencing the behavior. Our social conditioning also interferes with our perceptions and beliefs.

Humans have been conditioned to think, speak, and act in certain ways in situations. Now, you have the conscious ability to override that conditioning to change, grow, and manage the chaos within you.

Are you denying you have Free Will? Or are you beginning to understand YOU ARE energy with *Conscious Abilities*?

Chapter 4: The Heart

Attitude— a feeling or way of thinking that is expressed through your behavior. You can have a bad / negative attitude, or you can have a good / positive attitude; your thoughts are your choice, remember, Free Will. So, attitude begins with a conscious thought. What is the motivation? It all boils down to one thing, the heart; with all your feelings. If you are unsure of what you are feeling at any time, just ask yourself, "Does this come from fear or love?" Remember, every other emotion is an extension of fear and love. Fear, anger, hate, frustration, nervousness, etcetera are good motivators (temporary) to give you the kick that you need to adjust your attitude and take action consciously and authentically.

The heart has an electromagnetic field - a field of force that consists of both electric and magnetic components, resulting from the motion of an electric charge and containing a definite amount of electromagnetic energy that can be measured outside of the human body. Simply stated, the conscious mind sends out thought energy, hitches a ride with the heart energy and extends beyond the human body? Remember, the mind and heart work together.

Have you ever walked into a room and felt a tension in the air? Have you ever become angry with someone because they were yelling at you? Have you ever felt like crying because someone else was crying? Have you ever been hugged by someone giving you their love and felt warm and full of love? Have you ever laughed so hard that your sides were hurting because everyone else around you were laughing that hard?... Congratulations, you have experienced *empathy*.

Do not confuse being sympathetic with being empathic; there is a difference. To be sympathetic to someone means you have a general understanding of what they are experiencing, and you show them compassion, providing comfort and reassurance. To be empathic means you feel their emotions, literally. If you have had a similar experience, then feeling their emotions will probably be even stronger. Empathy is the ability to feel other people's energies, or energies of a particular environment.

For those of you who can feel others that is a testament to your own self-awareness. Those who are wrapped up in their own ego may not be aware of what others are feeling, but their energy does have an effect on those around them. You do not have special powers. You have natural Conscious Abilities. Your awareness is special and uniquely your own.

Everyone is capable of being empathic. Most humans are unaware of what they feel might be coming from someone else. For those of you who are aware of what you are feeling from others, know that there is a way to manage it. First and foremost, you must recognize and own up to what YOU are feeling, your own emotions and physical body. You must be consciously aware of yourself, your authentic self.

By being the true self, aligning your mind and heart with your actions (authentic core); knowing what belongs to you, it becomes easier to recognize what belongs to someone else. Some people are so in tune with their empathic abilities, they are able to identify physical pain and the exact body part where the pain is located.

Animals have their own emotions and sense it from others. Those of you who notice that animals are drawn to you, we bet you have a lot of love in your heart and great kindness to animals. Plants, on the other hand, are a little different. They do not have a heart or the same sensory systems that humans and animals have. However, scientists have been studying the reaction of plant life to human thoughts. It is still unclear how plants sense our thoughts and emotions, but plants do react to pain and thoughts of harm.

So, instead of attempting to explain, compartmentalize, and analyse WHY you have the ability to feel other people. Hone in these skills. The ability to understand what another person is feeling gives you the ability to make a positive change in the world. Also, note that just because you can feel what someone else is feeling does not mean you have to allow those feelings to consume you. You have the choice to transform what you feel into something positive and send it back. Return to sender with love, from the heart. Be the change.

The Purpose of Empathy

What is the purpose of empathy? What is the purpose of having the ability to feel how other people are feeling? The sole purpose of empathy is to eventually move into awareness and practice of unconditional love for all humans on earth. Regardless of race, language, religion, status, or creed. We are all one. The ability to pick up and feel the emotions of others, both the positive and negative emotions of others only leads us to eventually feeling complete compassion for every human being on earth.

By knowing and feeling that every human will experience both good and bad emotions... Empathy awakens within a person the ability to see each and every person they ever meet in this life as an extension of themselves. Bringing the individual into a greater understanding that we are indeed, as humanity, all one. If we are at the core of our being living authentically, all united as one, we would feel the need to do no harm or bring about negativity to another person.

From the perspective of oneness, we would be more willing and move to spread more peace, love, and happiness to each person we encounter, as these are energies, we too at the end of the day wish to experience for ourselves as well.

The gift of empathy, therefore, provides one with the never-ending desire to want to put into practice the golden rule: "Do unto others what you want others to do unto you."\

The world, however, is not always loving and positive. There are instances, where you too must learn to recognize and manage your own emotions and protect your energy field. The proper use of protection of your own energy field will lead to the overall wellbeing of your own health, mind, spirit, and body.

Once you can recognize and manage your own emotions, including your outward reaction to situations, you can learn to control your empathic Conscious Ability. It starts with creating a "shield" (for lack of a better term). The magnetic field of your heart, visualize it as an armour of light energy you can surround yourself with like a bubble that cannot be physically seen, only felt. It is your "personal space" that only those you allow to penetrate can get through.

Creating the "Shield"

Calm your mind (remember chapter 2) center yourself. Inhale through your nose and exhale through your mouth; taking long deep breaths. Much like what you would do in meditation.

You can do this with your eyes open or closed. Imagine the center of your hurricane, the chaos you pulled into the eye, that little glow that is the essence of your soul and push that light outward it is whichever color you choose it to be. Surround yourself with your light, visualize it enveloping you like a bubble. You can make the shield as thick as you would like it. After doing this, pay attention to how you are feeling,
physically and emotionally.

True Story:

Karate class: [some kids discussing if the twins can telepathically communicate]

Sensei: Some people can. Some can feel.

13yo: How can people feel?

Sensei: The heart's magnetic field can be measured outside of the body. So, if mine is out here [spreading arms] and yours is here [gestures to space] and the two connect then we could feel each other.
[note: they just had a moment of rest and 13 had not taken his turn on the pads, yet]

13: Ok, that makes sense.

Sensei: [Consciously scanning 13, from approximately 5 feet away and many other kids in close proximity... Heart beating faster, I felt nothing else] Why is your heart beating faster?

13: ... [Hand to chest] How did you know?!?

Sensei: I felt it.

13: HOW?

Sensei: I could not sense anything else. Do you have ANYTHING going on in your body? [Gestures to 13's whole body]

13: .... Nope. Nothing. [Contemplating what just happened]

Mind and Heart

It takes courage to operate in a balance between mind and heart. Most people lean towards using one over the other, social conditioning. However, the mind and heart when in unison working together can work wonders in a greatly beneficial way. Gone are the days of only being completely mind driven, or only completely heart driven. We are now entering a time and space where we are seeing humans combining both mind and heart energy in decision making, thus turning circumstances into better more favourable outcomes.

Everything you turn your attention to gives you an emotional response, which by your thoughts you choose your story. Your thoughts direct your attitude, your heart magnifies that energy sending it beyond your physical body. This means: Where you direct your attention, with your mind and heart, you are giving energy and attracting more of that same energy.

You are reading this. You are thinking about what you have read, and you may be feeling angry, skeptical, amused, curious... Think for yourself, you always have that choice (Free Will). What does your heart say? Is the answer coming from a place of anger / fear? Or do you feel the excitement with the desire to understand more? Either way, are you motivated?

Chapter 5: The Body - Living Authentically

Your physical body, the house for your conscious mind and heart energy, is also made up of energy.

"Quantum physics proves that solid matter does not exist in the universe. Atoms are not solid, in fact, they have three different subatomic particles inside them: protons, neutrons, and electrons. The protons and neutrons are packed together into the center of the atom, while the electrons whizz around the outside. The electrons move so quickly that we never know exactly where they are from one moment to the next."
(https://www.learning-mind.com/everything-is-energy/)

So, your thoughts, feelings, and body, are all energy. Anyone who has tried to stick two magnets together knows that the polarity of the magnet will repel the same charge and attract the opposite. Ah, but here is where it gets weird. In chemistry, like attracts like. When two bodies have like charges, and one has more force energy vibrating at different frequencies, then the force of attraction is greater than the force of repulsion.

This is how you attract what you think, feel, and do. You are putting your conscious energy out there, fuelled with the heart and put into action through the body.

When you are vibrating low in negativity, you attract more negativity, probably a life lesson to experience. In a vibrational state, you are repelling those who are unlike and attracting who are like. Heart energy coupled with consciousness is powerful, especially when it comes from love.

When you align your mind, heart, and live authentically with passion as the true you, you are putting out a higher force of energy, attracting a similar force of energy. Your perception and attitude ultimately determine the direction. The intention is the defining line. [*This is neither complete nor exact, this is an interpretation / perspective.*]

Your new understanding of thought energy and heart energy opens up a plethora of possibilities for you. The body is the vehicle to move the mind / heart energy, the third piece of the authentic self.

There is tremendous power in expressing yourself coming from both the mind and heart being in full alignment with each other. This power brings about a tremendous union with you and your authentic self, which naturally leads you to live a life fully authentic to your very core, the true you.

"I am who I'm meant to be, this is me
Look out 'cause here I come
And I'm marching on to the beat I drum
I'm not scared to be seen
I make no apologies, this is me."
(Keala Settle - The Greatest Showman Ensemble)

This authenticity is not the You that others want you to be, or the you that you think you must be to fit into social norms. It is the YOU that you have always known yourself to be, the YOU that feels true to you.

"Today you are You, that is truer than true. There is no one alive who is Youer than You." (Dr. Seuss)

This authentic self also leads to a better world. When you are in tune with your authentic self the inner world within you is clear, centered, and filled with pure intent. This is because your true authentic self comes from pure love. This pure love expressed outwards in your day-to-day life is what makes this world a better place.

Taking action from a place of love (your true essence) you are compelled to take action and good deeds for others, be kinder, be of help to others in need, or perhaps be more generous towards others. These small acts of kindness done on a daily basis are what is changing the world around you, as what you give out you get back. Therefore, the more people that come from and operate from this authentic self, in turn also continue to perform acts of kindness in their daily life as well, and the ripple effect grows and extends to a much better world to live in. Start to come from this authentic self, more in your day-to-day life and see how by changing that inner world, it does truly change your outer world.

If you are stuck in a low negative state-of-mind, change your routine. Random acts of kindness. Seriously, it takes the focus away from, "Me. Me. Me," and turns it towards love and kindness. Simple things to start with: hold the door open for a stranger, carry groceries in, take out the trash, compliments.

The authentic self is raw, real, inspired, and full of passion. This is the YOU that is and always has been meant to do great things in the world. This is the You that is set up in a manner that is guiding you for the full awakening of your very own inner greatness, expressed outwards into the world. Making this world a better place. The way you express this newfound unison between both thought and heart energy begins with communication.

Communication

Language is our human ability to speak to each other. Communicating through verbally / written, via body language face to face and technology (until we remember how to telepathically communicate). Your thought begins it, your heart amplifies it, and your physical actions increase the momentum. Every word you think / speak attached with your corresponding attitude, becomes a vibrational energy wave. The choice of words used directs the focus and presents the vibes of the message. When you focus on what not to do, even though you are saying, "Don't," you are in fact, giving attention to the very act of what has been said not to do.

For those times you do feel the need to express a negative choice, it can still be presented in a positive way. A simple example: "Don't touch. Wet paint." Which of course, focuses on "touch" and let us be honest, how many people still go ahead and touch the paint? What could be said instead, "Careful. Wet paint." This informs the person of the wet paint and focuses on being careful.

You can call this the Law of Attraction, or simply understand it is a basic language trick. The words you choose, and the emotions attached to those words become your energy. Amusingly, these same tactics work with kids. Not only are they learning from your example, only the focus words stick.

Some more examples:

Instead of "Don't forget" *use* "Remember to"

Instead of "I don't like" *use* "I like"

Instead of "Don't worry" *use* "Believe or Trust"

Instead of "I can't" *use* "I am"

Instead of "I hate" *use* "I love"

Make a conscious effort to change your choice of words, directing your focus to the positive. Give your attention to what you desire and wish to manifest into your reality.

It Starts with a Thought - Here is where you have to really get the words or image right. If you think "I need..." you will always need. If you think "I want..." you will continue to want. If you think "I have..." then you will have. It is already here. It is all in the words you choose to use, *like attracts like*.

Attitude Makes A Difference

People today generally are quick to complain about situations or a person they may be dealing with. It has almost become a default setting to focus on the negative. When you hear others say to "focus on the positive" they are not kidding.

You are going to get what you deserve, so check your emotions. Even people will be what you think them to be. If you call someone an idiot, then to you (your conscious observed perception) that is just what they will be. By calling someone smart or thoughtful, then you have given them the opportunity to rise up to that. With a positive attitude, you attract positive

Action

Are you one of those people that wishes they would win the lottery, but never buy a ticket? You have to go after your dreams. Talk to people. Grab hold of opportunities when presented to you. With the right attitude, you can make things happen. Absolute belief is the key.

It is really quite simple

Consciously practice using your words, having a good attitude, and putting it into action. Will it be challenging? Most likely. First of all, think in the positive and present / past tense with gratitude. If you believe it will not work, then you are correct that it will not work. But in that sense, it does work for the simple fact you believe it does not work that is what works. (Have fun wrapping your mind around that one).

Happiness is a State-of-Mind

Living authentically begins with a happy state of mind. Living a positive life is a choice you can make. The way you perceive situations and the attitude you carry with you is your decision. There is that Free Will again (it is yours). You are probably wondering how a person can just decide to be happy; it is really quite simple. Is it easy? No. It is something that does take a conscious effort, a little work, and a whole lot of practice. But just like anything that is worth doing is going to take some effort. With enough conscious practice, eventually, it will become a natural response like breathing. Being the authentic self, you are in essence connecting back to authentic happiness, an extension of love, as well. Where does true happiness come from? Happiness flows from within your very being. As you focus on the good you attract more happy moments into your experience.

Gratitude

Be grateful for what you have. When you appreciate what you have, you can then begin to deserve your desires. Look around you. You have a place to sleep. You are wearing clothes. If you are reading this right now, then you have some sort of connection with the rest of the world. Consciously be grateful for the people in your life as well. When we focus on being grateful for people that have in some way helped, inspired, or made life a little bit easier for us we attract more of that same experience. By being grateful for the people in our lives, we attract even more people in our lives to be grateful for. What else do you have? What if you had less? Have some gratitude and appreciation for people, experiences, things… life.

Remember, what we are grateful for expands. This means that we can actually be grateful for events and experiences in advance as well. The ancients left instructions.

"Whoever has gratitude will be given more, and he will have an abundance. Whoever does not have gratitude, even what he has will be taken away from him." (Matthew 13:12)

"If you are grateful, I will surely increase you in favour." (Quran 14:7)

"It is better to light one small candle of gratitude than to curse the darkness." (Confucius)

"...ingratitude is injustice and the greater the benefit received the greater the injustice done if gratitude is not given." (Socrates)

"Give thanks for unknown blessings already on their way." (Native American Saying)

PLOT TWIST! Here is the sense of humour in energy attraction. Your *INTENTION*, that little whisper in your conscious thought is deciding the motivation you attach to your gratitude. You will attract back exactly what you deserve.

This is the power of having gratitude in advance for things, experiences, or people you want to manifest into your life. Now that you are beginning to be grateful for what you have you have already begun to shift your thoughts to the positive and your heart to love. How you phrase things also makes a difference. Choose your thoughts and words carefully. Instead of saying, "I hate it when..." it is much better to focus on what you like or love about something.

Consider, "I love it when..." Your attitude and perception is always your choice. By focusing on what you love, you will attract more of what you love. Your thoughts begin it, your emotions amplify it, and your actions increase the momentum.

And you are on your way to living a positive life. What else can you do to make it better? Are you going to stress over things that already happened? Or stress over things that have not happened yet? You are writing your story; so, enjoy what is right there in front of you in the present time. Live in the moment. Stress - "The confusion created when one's mind overrides the body's basic desire to choke the living daylights out of some jerk who desperately deserves it." We have all experienced this frustration. That moment you want to completely lose yourself and physically express what you are thinking and feeling...

The best way to enjoy those moments is to laugh. Laughing is the physical response to joy. Love, with its counterpart, nervousness. Laugh as often as possible. Laughter is the best medicine for the soul. Laughter also raises your vibes as it overrides all other emotions. If something goes wrong in your day, find the humour in it. Almost anything can be found to be funny. It is all a matter of how you view things. Shift your perspective.

Yes, things are going to come up, little issues that might rattle you (social conditioning). Shrug it off and go with the flow. Sometimes things happen to change your path; just roll with it. If you can change the situation, then handle it. Believe that everything will work out. You may be amazed at where it will lead you. It IS your choice.

Are you laughing, rolling your eyes and thinking, "[-*fill in the blank*-]?" …Would you like a simple interpretation of the science? We now know, thoughts are vibrational energy, the heart is influenced by the thoughts and has higher vibrational energy. Your heart's magnetic field extends out beyond your body. Take the energy of your thoughts and attach your heart / emotional energy, (the closer to love the higher the vibrations) that is a lot of charge going out, attracting back the same. Remember, in chemistry like attracts like. When two bodies have like charges, and one has more force energy vibrating at different frequencies, then the force of attraction is greater. We are combining conscious thought with heart energy and interacting with other conscious observers. Energy cannot be destroyed, but it can be changed from one form to another.

Living authentically, (your interpretation of who YOU Are is your choice). Remember, those things that come up to shake you off your center are there for you to learn (gives you a gauge on your feelings, too) and at some point, you had attracted it to you. You could analyse your life and find the correlations to what you were thinking with what you experienced.

Or learn from your life experiences, consciously make an effort to communicate in a more positive direction, be aware of the charge of energy you are vibrating out through your attitude. Because it is coming back around. Complaining attracts more of what you are complaining about, fix it and change your perspective. Gratitude attracts more things for you to appreciate. You are creating your life.

Your experiences, your attitude, your thoughts are all your own. Free Will gives you the power to direct and manage your thoughts, heart, and body. Be consciously aware, motivated with passion. Do you feel that spark? That motivation to understand your Conscious Abilities?

Chapter 6: Consciously Directing Your Life

Intriguing? Are you following, so far? Your entire Being: mind, heart, and body is energy. Motivated (charged) by the heart. Your conscious awareness of Free Will gives you the Conscious Ability to choose the direction. The energy you put out with your thoughts, charged with your heart and put into action through your body, become a force of energy that is attracting the same charge. The cycle repeats until a conscious observer interferes and changes the behavior of the energy force, meaning you choose to learn a lesson and alter the direction and charge, attracting a new likeness.

Energy cannot be destroyed, it can only be shifted, transformed, altered, or redirected (First Law of Thermodynamics). You have been attracting energy back to you for a long time. Manifesting your life with your thoughts, attitude, and choice of actions. Have you been kind? Compassionate? Love is the most powerful of the heart's energy.

If you have been in this (above example), loving and compassionate in your energy space for most of your life, you will see that in your current life experience now, you also tend to also attract the same back to you in the form of people being kind and compassionate. Or you may find experiences in your life, where kindness and compassion of others also show up in mysterious ways.

With this in mind. There is a residual delay in the energy attraction, depending on what you are ready to receive. Think about it. We humans have scattered ourselves all over the globe. It can take some time for events and things to align. Manifesting is not as if you materialize an item out of nothing before your eyes.

At the time you think about something, it already exists. Connecting with you on a physical level takes time. Time is merely a construct of perception. A conscious way of measuring and organizing thoughts. Some of those energetic connections are already entangled with you. Quantum Entanglement is when a group of particles share the same behavior even when they are physically separated at a distance. So, now you know, your thoughts and heart energy have a never-ending effect.

The never-ending energetic attraction and entanglement can easily be explained with Karma, a Sanskrit word meaning "action," is regarded as a law of absolute universal justice. You are attracting the same thoughts / heart energy / actions that you have generated out into the world, returning to you with more force. And since energy cannot be destroyed, it would make sense that your conscious mind would transfer to another "state of being" after its "house" became deceased.

What is the biggest fear-based motivator with most human beings? The fear of death. Why are you afraid if your energy cannot be destroyed? Consciousness continues, possibly repeats life experiences. Because of quantum entanglement. Same conscious, same thought patterns, same energy attractions, a new perspective, new life lessons, new experiences, growth.

The return time of your thought and heart energy will vary, some will be instant while others may take years to come to fruition. Once you are aware of this, you will notice more and more synchronicities. If you have spent years complaining, focus on the negative perspective. That is a lot of negative energy returning to you. You have to shift that energy and to a positive charge. Be patient. Good things will come.

Remember, bad things happen to give you a gauge to know what is good and to give you a reason to appreciate experiences. It also brings out your truest strengths. You attract it, maybe not in this lifetime, but at some point, you do. The return time allows you opportunities to learn your lessons and change the behavior. Furthermore, would you consider it a bad experience if in the bigger picture, you are growing through the experience? If something is challenging or painful at any moment in your life, those are also the same moments that great opportunities for your growth in a positive direction arise; those are the moments that help you discover your strengths.

"Contrary to popular misconception, karma has nothing to do with punishment and reward. It exists... to teach us responsibility for our creations-and all things we experience are our creations."
(Sol Luckman)

"How people treat you is their karma; how you react is yours."
(Wayne Dyer)

The thoughts you think create the actual experience that you will have by shaping your perception. The universe flows to you and blesses you with all the goodness, joy, love, abundance, and positive experience based on the energetic signal you are sending out. What you send out you get back.

Imagine what you can do with your life once you understand that you create it with how you think. This understanding of having the ability to create the life you want, by what you think is powerful. From this perspective and this model of thinking you are placed in the driver's seat of your life. You are in essence choosing to no longer be the victim and instead of becoming the victor in any situation you are faced with in your life. Tuning into your authentic self, you come from a place of empowerment and are able to do amazing things in the world. This is also known as consciously manifesting your reality.

Consciously Manifesting

If you are going to manifest your dreams. Go big! Forget about HOW it manifests, simply put that thought and heart energy out there, remember to Believe, seeing and feeling the gratitude as if it is already there.

The Power of Having Gratitude in Advance

Let us say you would like to manifest a trip around the world. It has always been your dream, to explore different cultures and new countries. The problem is at this time you currently have no idea how it will happen. What if each day you started to be grateful in advance for already having travelled around the world. What would that feel like? Get into the emotion of gratitude of already being in that end goal of already having travelled the world as if it already happened.

An example of good gratitude in advance - affirmation for this specific manifestation would be: "I am so happy and grateful now that I have just travelled the world, and I am overwhelmed with gratitude for this experience taking place." Feel the gratitude and also visualize yourself already having completed your travels to your favorite destinations. You will be amazed at how powerful this manifestation technique works. You can use the gratitude in advance manifestation technique for whatever you want to manifest whether it be more abundance, landing a job/starting a business, manifesting a specific person/people, or manifesting favorable circumstances or your choice. What you are grateful for in advance, will manifest into reality.

Taking Action to Manifest Your Dreams

Opportunities will be presented to you. What you do with it is your choice. Have the courage to step out of your comfort zone and grab hold of opportunities. Take the steps toward your dream; plan that trip. How would you choose to travel and to where? Write out your plan. Get your funds in order, book that trip. Get your passport, start packing. Most importantly, get moving, spread kindness, and live with passion.

Your energy is interacting with others and continuously sending out your thoughts and heart energy, attracting more of the likeness. What you do every moment has an energetic impact and changes with every thought. How are you affecting the world? Is it positive? Is it kind? What you think, say, feel and do in your everyday life is where you can truly make a difference, for yourself and everyone else.

When it comes to living authentically, taking action from a pure place that comes from love, kindness and positivity go a long way, to bring back even more love, kindness, and positivity back to you. You will notice that your actions come back around to you. When does it come back around? It depends on your karma in this lifetime.

Understanding your karma in this lifetime is the key factor that your authentic self needs to learn most about in this current lifetime. Quantum entanglement or karma is the reason that most Conscious souls choose to come back on earth. What you do in this lifetime or (don't do) comes back to you in some form, and you repeat the life lesson until you learn it and get it right, so you can move onto the next level of your conscious evolution.

With this understanding of your karma and knowing what your authentic self needs to learn the most, doing what it takes to balance out your karma, is key to the turning point to bring you back to your full power, thus bringing you back to your authentic self.

One way to balance your karma is to <u>accept personal accountability</u>. If you make a mistake, own it. Live with love. Be aware of your thoughts and what you are attracting back. Learn your lessons. Eventually, your past karmic energy will have caught up to you. Life is like one big classroom. You are a student in this thing called life, here to learn lessons. Some lessons are challenging, and some lessons are easier than others. In order to advance to the next level, you have to learn the lessons that you are faced with in your here and now. The good news is that you have unlimited potential and conscious free will to navigate through the lessons, ultimately it is your choice.

Did we completely lose you or are you beginning to understand the unlimited potential your conscious Free Will, mind, and heart are capable of experiencing? Are you concerned with what your friends, family, and society might think if you decided to change your attitude? If you decided to live authentically?

Chapter 7: Living Authentically - Using the Tools You Have

Along this journey of tuning back to your authentic self, you may find that other people start noticing you behaving differently and will almost always have something to say about this new change in you. This can go both ways, maybe people compliment you in a positive way on this newfound self that has emerged within you, maybe others negatively criticize you for this change. The opinions of others will almost always come into play, with any new changes you make in your life.

You may encounter this, and it may feel uncomfortable at first. Yet, at the same time, you feel a sense of liberation with who you are and meant to be in this world. Once, you practice living more authentically, you will start to see people that are at your vibration draw closer to you. People that have connected to their authentic self will be excited and in awe simply by your very presence, simply because you are mirroring back the energy (light) from you to them and vice versa.

As the saying goes. *The light within me honours the light within you.*

This further amplifies your authentic lifestyle and creates an even more positive experience that is lining up with your authenticity, bringing more confidence and more of a shine to your way of being.

Peer pressure can be a motivator to get you moving. But only if you truly choose what your peers are choosing. Have the courage to be different. Dare to be YOU. Remember those who are not on the same vibrational wave of energy as you will repel / rebel. Just as you will with others. How you deal with these people is your choice, your test, and your life lesson. Every interaction you have, be it great or small, has an effect on you. Your awareness gives you the choice as to how you use it to grow.

Some people will cross your path with a whisper, some will strike you like a bolt of lightning, and others will leave a deep imprint on your heart. All of them will have an impact on who you are becoming. Number one thing to remember is that NO ONE can MAKE you think, feel, or do anything. They can compel you or trigger an attitude, or motivate you with fear, but How you react is Your Choice and your karma.

What Does it Mean to Be Authentic?

The definition of your authenticity is how you choose to define it. The paradox is, the more you attempt to define and label yourself attempting to "fit" in, the further you drift from your true self. These labels are words for communication, the doorway to your classroom for life. Your authenticity is who you really are with your mind and heart (love base), expressing yourself through your actions. Sending out your energy in vibrational waves. Your actions increase the power of your energy (remember it is coming back around another time).

When you take action from a place of compassion (an extension of love), how does that feel compared to how it feels when the same action comes from a much lower vibrational state? Acting out of anger or sadness (lower vibrational states) may serve as a temporary motivator but your body takes the hits (remember the thoughts-affect-water experiment). And the karma (attracting return energy) will come back around; a lesson you still need to learn, to have some compassion - energy powered by love from the heart directed by the conscious mind.

"The highest realms of thought are impossible to reach without first attaining an understanding of compassion." (Socrates)

The conscious mind would have no motivation without the heart. The energy from the heart has the highest vibrational frequency with pure love. The lower the frequency, the denser your energy and the slower you will move. Your body will especially feel the impact of lower vibrations over time. The good news, however, is that when you are in that lower vibrational state, you can discover it sooner with practice, through self-awareness.

For instance, you may recognize that you are in a lower frequency, and yet as a little bit of time passes you will have the ability to change your thoughts into gratitude, putting it into action with kindness, and thus remember to love yourself and have compassion for yourself overriding thinking and feeling from that lower vibration.

When you have compassion for yourself, after dipping into lower frequency you train yourself to be kinder to yourself. That true compassion starts with you first. Onc thing that is extremely powerful is that moment you realize you are slipping into a lower frequency vibration / negativity. Instead of beating yourself up for it, try in that moment moving back into a mental / heart space of gratitude. What are you grateful for in that moment?

Can you mentally and emotionally run through people, things, events in your life that you are grateful for? Maybe you are grateful for your good health, your relationships going smoothly, or any event that recently took place and you are happy.

Remembering to be grateful for moments when you find yourself slipping into a lower vibration, is very helpful in raising your vibration. This will allow you to be a lot kinder to yourself. This kindness to yourself that you practice, brings you back to the energy of love within.

By coming back to that center of love within you, you can then move into actions more aligned with your authentic self, which IS love. Actions, originating from love is how this world becomes a better place. Imagine when everyone on the planet becomes aware of this knowledge and practices this daily. It begins with YOU.

With the world WE humans created in its current state, there will be challenges / lessons. Your Conscious Abilities give you the power to make things shift to a positive charge - higher vibrations.

As you interact with others, you are moving that energy. Interacting with kindness and compassion increases the power with a positive charge. You do not have to agree with a person to be kind. You express your authenticity while allowing them space to express theirs. If you are not a vibrational match, repel with love.

Practicing and Using the Tools

The most convenient tool available to the conscious mind is the body, allowing you to express yourself and experience life in the physical. Humans have the desire within them to be happy, live peacefully, and are making an effort, sometimes.

The whole idea of sending out positive energy is why many people get involved in group meditations. It has been proven that when a group focuses and meditates with their hearts "cleansing" the world, there is a positive shift in the empathic atmosphere.

Group meditations are a great way to shift the world's energy. However, what you think and do after the meditation session will make a greater and longer-lasting impact. Many people who participate in a group meditation or attend religious gatherings (which is also a form of group meditation), get in sync with the crowd, fill the space with love; and then return to their daily life patterns with a completely different attitude.

If you find yourself screaming at your kids, spouse, or siblings, yelling angrily at a driver who cut you off, or even holding a grudge against your neighbour because their tree is over your fence line, then you will be counteracting any positive energy created during a "group meditation."

Are you creating hate and anger energy? Or are you creating love and compassion?

When you go out into public, be aware of your energy, your thoughts, and your feelings. Make a mental effort to send out good vibes. You can walk around smiling, giggling, and humming under your breath, you can do this openly or discreetly, as you feel your energy spread out. By the way, smiling, laughing, singing, dancing, and any exercise are a few physical ways to raise your own vibes. You can help make a difference just by keeping your own positive energy up and help to raise others. This does not mean you have to be that bubbly, cheerful person, just BE YOU.

You send out an energetic field that affects the world around you. With that heart energy, you have the power to change YOUR world.

Mindfulness

The practice of mindfulness in your daily life can enhance the quality of your life and align you with your authentic self. Your everyday actions can be a form of meditation. Active meditation occurs while being aware, appreciating details in your daily actions. For instance, while you are walking to your destination, slow down and pay attention to how your body moves with each step, how you are breathing, what you are feeling both physically and emotionally. Absorb the details of your surroundings. When you take a shower, notice how the water feels, the temperature, the soap suds washing away any negativity. The same could be done when hand washing dishes. Everything you do, slow down and really pay attention, all of your senses may come alive as you appreciate more and more details.

Everyone eats. It is something most people take for granted. *Mindful eating* is an absolute must.

1.) Consciously be grateful for your food. Express your gratitude.
2.) Look at your food, notice the colors, aromas, textures, the presentation.
3.) As you take a bite and chew your food, allow your tongue to enjoy the flavors, notice the textures, how it feels when you swallow.
4.) Be grateful.
5.) Have a conversation with the people around you. Meals are meant to be shared.
6.) Be grateful.

By giving your attention to the details, appreciating the moment, you allow clarity and flow.

Understanding Your Triggers

The first few years of the child's life can bring triggers into adulthood that spiral the adult into a negative vibrational flow spiral. These triggers can come in the form of trauma. These traumas if left unhealed will bring more pain to the adult and this is the cause of so much disharmony in the world. What can one do to release these triggers?

Some find conventional therapy (consulting a licensed therapist) as a means of healing deep childhood past wounds. Some just learn to deal with it and never really heal. While some choose to become aware of the triggers and forgive themselves and everyone, they believe caused the triggers. One way of transforming from your trigger is to recognize the emotional pain.

Actually, sit with the pain for a bit. This is extremely uncomfortable and not easy. It is a process that takes some people longer to handle than others.

Then ask yourself why this pain is still helping you, the only reason for holding onto emotional pain is because in some way you believe it is helping you in some form. After sitting with that pain, for a minute or two. Can you at that moment release that pain, and come to a place of self-awareness where the pain is no longer hindering you? Can you release the trigger by acknowledging it, feeling it, and then letting it go.

Forgiveness is the Ultimate Tool

Your past is where we can find your true authentic self. The most powerful tool to discovering your authentic self is by doing what we will call a complete reset. This means going back to your past where the trigger was created with the original trauma, and then forgiving yourself and everyone involved who you believe caused that trauma to happen. This process is difficult for most people, as most aren't willing to do this deep work within themselves, because the mere thought of the pain or trauma caused at a very early age is well, too painful. Those that are willing to go through this process of healing through forgiveness, however, do come out of it with a sense of clarity of purpose and realigned back to their true authentic self.

It is quite a simple technique. You simply go into a deep meditation and go back to where that trauma or pain took place. Then consciously relive it, feeling it happening again. You choose (when you are ready) and say, "I forgive you."

Say this as you mean it, with feelings of compassion in your heart, knowing that anything in your past can be completely healed through love. And think of all those that you feel may have wronged you during that time that enhanced the trauma and say the same thing over and over again. "I forgive you."

Remember, forgiving others for the pain or hurt they caused you is not always easy. But, in doing so you are actually helping yourself even more than the other person. By forgiving those that hurt you, you are setting yourself free. That does not mean what they did was not wrong, or a mistake. It means you are willing to be free from that control of holding onto past pain from further affecting your choices and actions from here on out.

This process of forgiveness is a tool you can use every time you feel out of alignment with your authentic self. Maybe there is some residue from your past that you need to really just forgive, then let it all go.

Mentally and emotionally forgive. Let it all go. You will find this process to be very healing and powerful, and when done correctly life changing. Healing is a process. And with all of the things going on in your life it can be challenging to keep your focus on what you are attempting to heal and create in your life. Sometimes, something tangible can help you to remember to hold that focus.

The Power of Belief

The Placebo Effect - has proven that belief is a powerful agent in healing the mind. We are not prescribing medication to help you, that is up to your doctor. We are suggesting believing in your own power. Stones and crystals are Tools to help you focus. Before you roll your eyes, understand the science.

The gemstones have their own vibrational properties, just as all things do (everything is energy). The stones are not magic, actually more like magnifiers. Also, stones and crystals serve as reminders to the conscious mind to awaken the same vibrational properties within themselves. And you have to admit, the stones are pretty.

How it works is similar to using a lucky penny or pair of lucky socks. The bearer of said item believes the item is lucky and therefore, has more confidence and believes in themself. By attaching a thought or belief to a specific stone, you are giving yourself something to direct your focus, magnifying that energy with a vibrational match. The belief is why it works. Even with everything else going on around you, that little reminder is tucked into your mind generating more energy. Touching the stone solidifies the connection because now you have involved your body with the mind. Believing completes the trinity with the heart, your authenticity.

For instance, it is said that when you wear a jade necklace when you sleep, you will remember more of your dreams. If you decide to try this, you are consciously telling yourself to remember your dreams and the necklace is your reminder, the tool to help you direct your focus. You can search the world wide web for the vibrational properties of each stone to find the one that you feel is a vibrational match for your purpose of using the tool. Just FYI quartz crystal is a general, all-around useful focusing energy tool.

Are you getting how all of this works together? Being authentic (thoughts, emotions, actions), living with compassion and gratitude, releasing your past, living in the moment, believe, love… We are giving you a map to navigate your life, you choose your path. On your path, you will have guides. Are you paying attention?

Chapter 8: The Flow State and Receiving Signs

While on your journey to aligning with your authentic self, there are two things that will start to occur in your life.

Firstly, you will find yourself in the flow state a lot more often.

Secondly, you will be receiving a lot more signs that you are on the right path.

Let us start by defining what it means to be in a flow state. To be in flow can have various meanings. For energy purposes, it means you are on your path, living authentically.

You can be in flow with routines, mindfully and smoothly completing tasks. Flow state is when you are fully engaged in any actions that require intense focus, as you are also fully immersed in the present moment. This state of being fully immersed in the present moment may feel like time is standing still. A feeling of complete oneness with you and the activity you are engaged with. There are occasions, however, when you get used to the routine, it is comfortable.

Doing the same thing each day without any changes to your environment and actions can bring stagnation. Eventually, your energy becomes stagnant and you find yourself bored more often. To reawaken your energy, flip your routine, step out of your comfort zone. Once in a while, a good practice to remember is to flip your routine.

"How do I flip my routine?"

If you normally go out at night, stay home. If you are an avid reader, watch a movie. If you are an avid movie watcher, read a book. (Oh hey, you are right now). Maybe you love to go hiking. Go to a museum. By doing something completely opposite of what is your normal routine, on occasion, you reboot your mind and heart. When you go back to your normal routines, you will have a new appreciation for what you love to do. And a new perspective because you had a different experience. Growth.

Synchronicity

You may have heard of the term, "Synchronicity," but do you really understand what it means? Most will tell you it is a random chance of events. Your life has taken you through twists and turns, ups and downs, gained many lessons learned, and an extensive amount of knowledge. Would you be the soul being you are without that knowledge and experience?

"Everything happens for a reason." A familiar phrase that defines the way synchronicity operates. At the energy level, every conscious soul with Free Will is weaving a massive web of energy. The chemistry and we humans keep it going. Once you understand and accept the concept of synchronicity the signs are much easier to recognize.

Humans like to give identities to idealisms; it would suggest that humans need something tangible to believe in and to help make sense of what they do not understand. Some people believe it is spirit guides performing these small acts of synchronicities, some say it is angels or fairies. In Your version of reality, it is a reflection of what is in your mind and heart. You attracted it. Either way, it happens. You will recognize the signs and you will interpret the message in a way that you understand and receive. Because of that thought, that desire to achieve, while you are living mindfully you will notice little things that are giving you some direction. If your heart agrees with it, there you go. Here is your path.

Synchronicity is responsible for seeing your normal route being blocked off because of construction work ahead, and you have to detour around the construction roadblock to take a longer route to your destination. You then arrive at a later time causing you to run into an old friend, which you would have missed had you arrived on time.

Or maybe you are on the road and you happen to be behind a driver who is driving extra slow. Maybe they are there to slow you down, making you miss an accident. Injuries as well as having a cold or flu are a big clue telling you to slow down, change your behavior, and pay attention.

Receiving Signs and Messages

When you are centered, living mindfully, you may notice certain phrases or other random "signs" that you consciously connect with whatever issue or project that is occupying your mind, remember your heart will tell you if this is true for you. It could come from a song on the radio, something someone says (directly to you or overheard), a literal sign you might see out and about, or even an event that you experience. Have you ever heard a particular song in your head come in out of the blue? Maybe the song keeps playing over and over again in your mind. If you pay close attention to the lyrics of the song, you will see that it is your subconscious mind pointing you in a certain preferred direction. Messengers come in many forms. It is all energy you are authentically attracting back to you.

If it encourages you to tap into your own innate inner power, provides a positive and thought-provoking outlook and/or motivates you to take action with love, then it is a good message. If it does not, move on.

The reason for receiving signs in your reality is to give you a little nudge to remind you to continue to move forward on your path (the project that is occupying your mind). To trust the process, as it is leading you to incredibly positive outcomes that you are manifesting.

The messages are there to confirm you are on your path. But synchronicity also happens to redirect your path, to get you in alignment with the energies you are consciously manifesting. Maybe that old friend you just ran into is someone you have been wanting to reconnect with. You never really know which way it is going to go. Does it matter which way? No, just follow your heart and go with the flow. Believe and be grateful.

Joy and Alignment

There is one particular emotion that gives you a good indication that you are aligned with your authentic self. This emotion is high vibrational energy. This one emotion (an extension of love) that shows if you are aligned with your authentic self is the emotion of joy. When you are feeling joy, this is the way to show you that you are on the right path. When you are filled with the emotion of joy that is a good indication that you are in the flow and on doing the right thing in your life.

When you are feeling good, feeling positive about life, and moving with the flow of joy it will feel amazing, just know that is a clear indication that you are heading in a good direction in your life.

The key here is to start becoming aware of those times when you are most joyful. It is different and unique for everyone. Whatever actions you are engaged in when you are feeling the most joy is an indication of what you are meant to be doing in life that is leading you to your soul's purpose.

Also, you use your emotions as a guide (personal GPS) to know if you are on the right path. Ask if you are on the right path. Is there an effective way to actually get some signs to show up in your life? Yes, and it is quite simple. Simply ask for signs. Try this out, take 3 deep breaths. Center your mind and body on your breathing.

Simply place both your hands on your heart and ask the question out loud in silence. "Please, give me a clear sign that I can easily understand to see if it is in my best interest to [-*fill in the blank*-]?"

After you have asked this question, simply release it. Forget about it and go about your normal day. Detach completely from the outcome. Detach especially of "how the sign or where the sign should appear." Simply trust that it will show up, and the sign will. Keep in mind, the lesser the resistance you have to how, where, when, and why the sign appears, the faster the sign shows up.

This does take practice. Sometimes, you may not get a sign immediately. However, if you tune in enough times and practice mindfulness, slow down, and pay attention, the signs that you witness as you go about your day, start to become clearer and clearer.

A lot of times using your own intuition already has the answers that you are seeking, looking for signs in the outside world in your external environment, simply serves as confirmation that you are indeed on the right path. If you are in-flow.

In the Flow State

Do you know those times where everything seems to be going your way? You feel light and joyful as if you are gliding through the day, as opposed to bumping into things and knocking things over. Karma can be pretty instant when you are in this flow state of being. When you go out driving, think "All green lights." This only works if you are staying at the speed limit. Slowing down and paying attention to mindful driving. When parking, think, "Space open, close to the entrance." All the while, holding on to that feeling of joy.

You are in tune with the energies around you. Your focus is in the moment directed towards your goal. You are grateful and joyful. And you are authentic, calm, centered and motivated because you are on your life path. The world around you appears to open up for you in magical ways. You become aware of other abilities like your "gut feelings" are seemingly accurate.

An Anonymous Police Officer shares his story and perspective:

"We all, as humans, get 'hunches' or. 'gut feelings' from time to time, and they turn out to be right a disproportionate amount of the time. Some people are more finely tuned to these feelings; we know them more readily when they strike and some of us can read them as we could a printed page in front of our eyes. It takes subtly different forms for each of us, but in an attempt to put too fine a point on it, that is what it is.

I am a police officer. I set out on this path. Early on in my career, I noticed things. While walking foot patrol, I would pick up on things and notice tones of voice and patterns of movements. These things would jump out at me no matter how much was going on in the background. A bar owner in the area I patrolled commented to me that he and other business owners liked me because, as he put it, "when something happens, it's like you come out of the wall and right into the middle of it." Now, with years of experience under my belt and a better understanding of my abilities, I will sometimes picture a specific place in my mind and go there, only to find myself in the middle of a fight or some other criminal activity.

I'm not a wizard, not a warlock, not an alien being. I am just a cop who is in tune with his gut, who knows the energy of the city he protects, and who senses things others might not. And so, it is with you in the path you have chosen in your own life.

Why do I feel this is important? If we are going to serve humankind, to make this world a better place for humankind, we must do it from within, not from without. If you wish to serve humanity, the best way to do it is by being human." (Anonymous)

Chapter 9: Thriving with Passion

"...By being human." Three simple words, with so much power. Human, or Homo Sapien (Latin for "wise man"), is the only species (that we are aware of) on this entire planet with Free Will. You, and you alone, are unequivocally responsible for Your thoughts, emotions, and choice of actions. You are responsible for the energy you create and send out into the world. "By being human," you acknowledge your consciousness and accept personal responsibility for your choices.

In school, you are given lessons and then tests to see if you learned the lessons; to gain knowledge. Life teaches us differently. We are tested over and over again until we learn the lesson. With each life test, we gain experience. The wisdom you gain through experience and learning your life lessons guides you to make better choices and to create a better reality. *The world is made of dreams that were created into reality by people who dared to dream with passion.*

The Ancient Greeks did not write obituaries. They only *asked one question* after a man died: *Did he have passion*?

Passion is the driving force (extension of love) behind all the great things we see in humanity. Passion - (adj.) a strong or extravagant fondness, *enthusiasm*, or desire for anything.

From a worldly view, we can say that there are many things that we as humans can still do to drastically improve upon to make this world a better place. One way we can do that is by serving humanity. With passion, we can go the distance, we can make a lifelong effort to do good for humanity through service connected with one's life purpose.

When Passion Meets Purpose

Everyone has a life purpose; some discover it earlier than others. Some find it in the midst of some major tragedy or life-changing event that changed their life drastically. Maybe a major accident or loss of a loved one. These are life-altering events that change a person's mindset and beliefs forever. It is during those times one may find their life purpose. When finding your life purpose, you awaken to almost like being a brand-new person, filled with a passion and drive towards a cause or a lifestyle change that can be linked directly to fulfilling one's life purpose. This passion-driven purpose leaves the person feeling a lot more fulfilled because one is now committed to taking action on something that is much bigger than themselves, and that ultimately leads to a legacy.

And there are some people who discover their passion through extracurricular activities, arts, or sports, for example. What might begin as a hobby, evolves into a passion as the person gains more experience with wisdom.

"Wisdom, compassion, and courage are the three universally recognized moral qualities of men." (Confucius)

Have the courage to live a life of purpose. A life that you feel has a deeper meaning that goes beyond yourself. Strive for something bigger in your life. Imagine looking back towards the end of your life, feeling, and knowing without a doubt that you did everything you could to lead a life of purpose and that you did it with good intent and passion. Envision the difference you can make while you are here on earth. By discovering and living your passions and choosing to direct that powerful energy towards serving humanity, you choose to help leave this earth a much better place for many generations to come; after your legacy has been established.

How to Find and Follow Your Passion

Humans by nature are exceptionally talented and gifted creatures. From being gifted in the arts, and other highly creative ventures. Indeed, being a human being on earth nowadays and having many talents is not uncommon. But how many people are actually following their passions for a living? As a human living on this planet, it is increasingly difficult to find your passion, because of two reasons that have been observed and researched.

Reason # 1. In studying talented people through extensive observation, we have found that many Humans are so well skilled in so many things, that they have a hard time really channelling their energy and time into one or two highly focused passions. The phrase "jack of all trades and master of none," comes to mind.

Reason # 2. Every human has a very selected and specific talent or passion, but the environment they live in with the people they are surrounded by might not support that one special passion or gift they have to offer the world. The lack of support from family and friends is what prevents the human-being from thriving with their passion and making a living from it.

What we want to share with you, first of all, is that if you do have many things you are interested in and that it is important to really get your focus into one or two passions that you feel most called to do, and that potentially can also help you earn a living for yourself.

Use the grounding techniques described in chapter two to ground yourself, to tuning in to one or two of the passions you are most interested in, and work on them. If you are already gifted in one specific area, we would suggest that you continue to pursue it. You are encouraged to pursue it because we know that from personal experience if a person is consistent in the pursuit of his or her passion, they will make a life of success for themselves. A life of true fulfillment, joy, and abundance is granted to those that continue to pursue their passion.

Inspired Action

Take inspired action and surround yourself with like-minded people that share the same interests and passions as you to get some support and accountability going. You can find people within your niche that share similar interests as you. This way you gather support and share ideas to start thriving as a human. The key ingredient here is to muster up the courage within yourself to truly make what you are passionate about into success.

"Once you make a decision, the universe conspires to make it happen." (Ralph Waldo Emerson)

The ordinary becomes extraordinary when you put your heart into it. You make an impact when you share your passion with others.

You will be rewarded when you are proving to yourself that you have what it takes by the action steps you take to move forward with your passion. Learn to trust your inner compass. Trust that you are being guided by the powerful energy love generates, and allow the events, people, and resources that will manifest for you once you trust in yourself and start living and working on your passion. So, what if you have not found your passion yet. How do you find your passion? If you need some guidance in finding your passion try and experiment with some of the suggestions and tips below.

Finding Your Passion

1. Ask Around
You are not the only one with a passion and you are not the only one looking. Friends and family will have spent many years trying to find out who they are. They will be living their own dreams, enjoying their own passions, or struggling to find their way as much as you might be. So why not ask them? Give your friends a call/ text. Send them an email. Start-up a conversation about hobbies, dreams, aims, or goals. Your friends will probably be very happy to talk with you about the things they enjoy doing, and you might even gain some inspiration!

2. Aim for Variety

It is rare for someone to find their passion right away. Nowadays, we have so many choices that we are not likely to fall into the right place straight away. Do not let that bother you. Give many things a go. The more you try, the more chances you will have of liking something. If you are generally not an active person, sports are probably not your thing. Try cooking, arts, music, public speaking, charity work, DIY, and gaming. You have far more chance of working out what you like.

3. Give It Time

You will not come across your passion all of a sudden. It will take time, and it will take effort. The world's best footballer did not kick a ball once and realized his life was supposed to be about the game. The world's most passionate human rights campaigner probably did not know what they wanted to do by the time they were talking, and that next-door neighbour, with five children, did not know everything about parenting when their first child came along. We learn along the way. We try things out, we give things time, and we enjoy things once we have learned how with experience– but the journey can be very enjoyable, too. If something does not feel right at the start, keep trying for at least ten days – you might find that ALL it takes is a little bit of practice, with experience you will gain wisdom.

4. Volunteer Your Services

There can be no better way to find out if you're really passionate about something than to do it for someone else, without being paid or rewarded. If you think photography is for you, try standing in the rain for five hours taking photographs of someone's wedding day. If you are certain you want to change the face of politics forever, try delivering a thousand leaflets as part of your campaign. If you can get through the exhaustion, and still love what you are doing, you are probably on the right track.

5. Say "Yes"

A top tip now: always say "Yes". There are books and movies about this very concept. Saying 'Yes' will always lead to fantastic new experiences, and the more you experience, the more you will learn. If a friend invites you to a party, say, "Yes." You might meet someone that will have a real impact on your life. If your brother asks you to fix his computer, say, "Yes." Even if you cannot fix it, you will probably end up learning something new. If your sister asks you to accompany her on a tandem skydive...well, you get the idea! Say "Yes," and you will be trying new things. Say "Yes", and you will be making the most of life. Say "Yes", and You have a much higher chance of finding your passion and thriving!

Passion v Addiction

Addiction is self-centered and can steal your life away. Addiction is driven by compulsion; you just cannot help it. Passion is enrichment, enthusiasm, and gives life. Passion is driven by love; you are motivated to keep going. When you turn your passion into something that serves the good of humanity, you will have found your purpose.

It is absolutely acceptable to not have found your purpose. Are you making the effort? Are you using your Conscious Abilities to create your life and leave your legacy with passion?

Chapter 10: We Are One

Captivating? Recap: Everything is made up of atoms and atoms are energy. We could as much say you are an atom, metaphorically speaking. Your body is the neutron, your Conscious mind is the proton, and your heart's Abilities are the electrons. Attracting other atoms that match frequencies, repelling those unmatched. You are a consciousness with Free Will, powered by love, experiencing life as a human from one perspective.

Human beings have *less* than 1% differences in each individual human's DNA. That teeny-tiny 0.1% is the reason we do not look exactly alike. We are all on an average 99.9% the same, genetically. As diverse humans appear to be, we are one. At the subatomic level, we are all connected.

Quantum Entanglement Connects People

Albert Einstein called this phenomenon, "Spooky action at a distance." Atoms are at a micro-level. To understand this, we will explain it at a macro level. Imagine, two balls rolling down a hill. The balls bump into each other. One ball bounces a great distance from the other. A person comes along, sees one of the balls, kicks the ball, and the ball bounces away. The other ball also moves when the first ball is kicked, because both of the balls' energy is entangled with the other from their previous interaction. Now, imagine this at a micro-scale, with our atoms.

How does this phenomenon work in humans? Every human you interact with, especially those you spend a great amount of time with, you will pick up subtle behaviours and mimic them yourself, most often without realizing it. Behaviours like facial expressions, the way you speak, the way you move, your interests, and even how you feel emotionally. This would explain the bond between twins because their energy became entangled in the womb. Have you ever looked at someone when they were yawning and you yawned, too?

"We are part of this universe, we are in this universe, but perhaps more important than both of those facts is that the universe is in us. When I reflect on that fact, I feel big, because my atoms came from those stars. There's a level of connectivity - that's really what you want in life, you want to feel connected, you want to feel relevant, you want to feel like you're a participant in the goings-on of activities and events around you. That's precisely what we are just by being alive." (Neil DeGrasse Tyson)

Rituals, Ceremonies, and Traditions

The purpose of these is to unite people. To bring human beings together and share a common interest, quite often in celebration. Evidence of this can be seen throughout religious practices, observing / celebrating holidays and special events; Sunday Mass, weddings, birthdays, graduations are recognized examples. The feeling of community allows people a sense of connection and belonging. This amplifies one's feeling of being accepted. Feeling accepted or part of the group brings a sense of unity and empowers people towards a common goal. What are the most common experiences that bring people together?

Music Brings People Together

Music is a universal language. Every culture from the past to the present has some form of music, often associated with poetry / song. Whether it be to tell a story, to celebrate, dance, or sing together, synchronizing everyone to the rhythm. Studies have shown that humans have a dedicated part of the brain to process music, suggesting that music has an important function in our lives.

Music can touch a person's soul, reaching their deepest emotions. Even babies recognize the rhythm and will bop their heads along with the tune. When you go to a concert, you are sharing that experience with everyone around you. When groups get together and sing, they are sharing the passion of the music experience. Dancing to music furthers that experience to something we can all do and feel like we are part of something. Dancing also raises our vibes, producing endorphins, making us feel lighter and happier.

Cultures all over the world have their own style of music. It is forever evolving, as we connect and share music with each other. It has even been discovered that plants have their own form of song. Many animal species have a form of a song to communicate with each other. Music is part of nature and clearly, part of the human design, to unite us.

Food and Togetherness

Food also brings a sense of togetherness. Regardless of your choice of food or preference, when gathered with other people during a meal, this offers you the opportunity to connect with and socialize with those around the meal table. Researchers from the University of Oxford found there was a direct link between the number of times people eat with others and their satisfaction with their daily life. Their survey showed very clearly that the more often a person does sit down and eat with other people, the more likely that person is to be happy and have higher levels of satisfaction with their lives.

Socializing while sharing a meal experience with other people is great for an individual's physical and mental wellbeing, and social eating plays a vital role in connecting and bringing a sense of togetherness with other people.

Social Media

The invention of the telephone began this quest. As our technology evolved, we developed more ways to connect with people. The rise of social media sites and apps prove that humans have the desire to connect with others. We have an innate need to belong, to be accepted.

"It is easier to build strong children than to repair broken men."
(Frederick Douglas)

"It Takes A Village to Raise A Child," - a proverb that means an entire community of people must interact with the children so that each child can grow with experience in a safe and healthy environment while learning from the wisdom of their mentors. We also learn from children. Children see the world with such innocence and honesty, they are reminders to the rest of us to see the world through their eyes.

Humans are designed to work together, as a whole. Would you be the person you are today if it were not for those who mentored you as you grew up? Would you even know your strengths if it were not for the challenges you faced over the years?

Our consciousness is in a child-like phase. Experiencing life on earth as a human. Just like children, we learn to fear. A child runs, maybe falls down, they get a bruise or scrape and learn fear from the pain and experience. But that is their lesson to learn, to slow down and to learn how to use their body, to avoid falling.

Duality

"Simultaneously holding two or more contradictory beliefs, ideas or values." (Urban Dictionary) or the same thing but opposite, like two sides of the same coin. The true definition depends on the context in which duality is used. The ancient symbol of the yin yang depicts the nature of duality. For one side to exist there is an awareness of the opposing side. Light cannot cast its own shadow. And a shadow can only exist when light is present and blocked.

Because of your self-awareness with Free Will, you have the Conscious Ability to choose how you allow outside energies to influence you, you *choose* your reaction to conflict. Understanding the opposition is wisdom, and it comes with experience. In your heart, the duality of love and fear serves a purpose, or as some might perceive this relation in the duality of good and evil.

Fear, anger, and stress are good *temporary* motivators. These moments bring out your truest strengths. We are learning how to respond and deal with conflict. Opposition and conflict are sometimes necessary to learn a life lesson, and to discover your true strengths.

"You cannot truly call yourself 'peaceful' unless you are capable of great violence. If you are not capable of violence, you are not peaceful, you are harmless. An important distinction." (Unknown)

The one way to change the direction and momentum of a force of energy is to meet it with an opposite yet equal amount of force energy. To be able to overcome lower vibrations, you must be able to rise above it. Match the force energy with love.

We (humans) have the Conscious Ability to learn, grow, and adapt as we expand our wisdom through experience. We have the ability to feel others and our energy has an effect on everyone around us. We have developed ways to connect with others around the world. Humans are 99.9% the same. Collectively, we are one big organism. Your choices, your energy has an effect on the collective.

Thoughts and prayers actually do work, not by a deity, but simply by the energy behavior in the thoughts; the key is to attach the appropriate heart energy to those thoughts that are being consciously sent out. Receiving that energy, believing, and accepting it, increases your own energy.

The fact that we are all connected, really means that we can create a better world to live in. Why? Remember, the chapter where we discussed the idea of empathy? The fact that we can feel other people's feelings at any given moment, means we all feel similar pain and joys in life as a whole. With this in mind, what we want for others we also get back for ourselves. What we say and do for others comes back to us.

If we are kind to others, we are kind to ourselves. The concept of oneness means we can all consciously use our abilities to uplift the vibration of the planet together. One for all, all for one!! Uplifting society and humanity as a whole.

"I was no longer needing to be special because I was no longer so caught in my puny separateness that had to keep proving I was something. I was part of the universe like a tree is, or like grass is, or like water is. Like storms, like roses. I was just part of it all. I had my unique function to play." (Ram Dass)

Is the idea of us being separated from each other the reason for suffering? Most humans are programmed by society at an early age that as humans we are all separate. This illusionary world of duality ends up leading to unnecessary conflicts, which leads to continual suffering on the planet.

All the world's major wars are due to the false belief shared amongst humans that we are separate. When we humans awaken to the idea that indeed we are one. The question remains, who and what are we really all here struggling to fight against?

The idea that you are at a deeper level, that you are completely different than the next person is what causes the unnecessary conflicts of the world. The idea of comparing oneself to others is what keeps us in a battle within ourselves. This battle is ongoing and yet can be avoided by *practicing inner peace within ourselves first*, then outwards in our interaction with others. By acknowledging and practicing this idea of oneness, how much unnecessary conflicts in the world can end? How you perceive others is a direct reflection of something you see in yourself.

Oneness in Meditation

"Is there a way you can go into a *feeling* of oneness at any given moment in time?" There is something you can do on a daily basis, (there is more than one way to practice this). The practice of deep meditation can give us a feeling of oneness. The moment that you go beyond your thoughts you begin to move into an energy field of complete oneness with all that is and that ever will be. It is an energy space of complete and total stillness, which is the precise energy that is connected to everyone and everything on this planet. This is when you are no longer thinking of any thoughts and you are the one with all of life. Depending on how often you meditate, it will depend on the length of time you can spend in that (feeling space) of oneness.

Remember mindfulness? Living and breathing mindfully; actively making every moment a meditation, absorbing an appreciation in the beauty and details around you, also brings a sense of calming peace. When you go for a walk in nature, you feel your body connect to the earth, seeing, hearing, and smelling everything. You can feel the energy around you, you breathe it in. You feel connected because you allow yourself to BE in that moment, appreciating the experience. The more you can silence the chaos in you for longer periods of time each day, the more connected you become to the state of oneness of everyone and oneness of life.

By practicing deep meditation or mindful awareness of oneness, we can also access this space at any time we choose. From this space of being connected to this oneness, you are using your Conscious Ability to reconnect with your authentic self, and moving towards a better world for all to live in. Deep meditation practiced daily changes your inner world and thus affects your outer world in a very uplifting and positive way.

Through meditation that is where we can find the oneness within yourself. How does oneness feel? Feelings of being in complete peace, love, and complete bliss are some of the feelings that come from entering this space of deep meditation.

Raising the vibrational waves of humanity as a whole unifies and strengthens the energy to a higher vibrational level. Everything works in circles until a consciousness with Free Will changes the direction.

The more humans connect and authentically vibe together with love, through kindness and compassion, the higher the vibrations on the planet. Reviving the Earth and Humanity for generations to come. You are responsible for your legacy.

Are you returning for another lifetime? Or are you accepting responsibility for the energy you create? Could you? Will you?

Chapter 11: Humanity and Singularity

Is your mind blown yet? Wait for it… because we have some philosophical ideas that piece together all that we have discovered and understand. If you have read this far into this book, your curiosity is peaking. You are ready to open your mind.

What is the point of Living?

The ultimate question most 'truth seekers' seek simply is: What is the point of living? What is the whole point of life? We all know that there will come a time when we are no longer living on this earth. We are all going to die, eventually.

Our physical human suits will expire, but energy cannot be destroyed. Where does our consciousness go after the body is deceased? Why do we fear death? The fear of death keeps humans alive. The fear of the unknown is a motivator. What are you motivated to do? There are many beliefs world-wide, of where we go after life as a human.

Heaven and Hell

The duality of the Afterlife. Depending if you follow the "rules" or not you will get either eternal bliss or eternal damnation after you die. The key motivator with this belief is the fear of eternal damnation itself. Many cultures and religions have slightly different versions of this afterlife duality.

Reincarnation

Wash-rinse-repeat. The consciousness will return for another lifetime with all the attached unresolved karma energy from the previous life, new experiences from a different perspective. Under this idea, if you do good deeds (a good person) in this lifetime, you are rewarded in the next lifetime with a good life. If you do mostly bad deeds in this lifetime you will have a more difficult life the next time around. The motivator with this belief is to create energy that attracts more of the same that you wish to have in your next lifetime. Choosing your next life-time journey.

Nothingness

According to proponents of *Solipsism* belief, in this world, you are the only person who actually really exists, and the entire universe is only in your mind and a product of your own imagination. Therefore, when you physically leave this earth and die, the universe itself will completely cease to exist. Your consciousness will simply transfer to nothingness.

If you believe there is *nothing* after death, then you have nothing to lose. Except what you are currently creating and attracting back into your life. The motivator under this belief is the desire to live the best life possible, while we have one.

Aliens

What if Earth is an experimental colony for an alien species? Or several alien species? Could our consciousness be from another dimension? Sent to earth to experience life as a human, with all the trials, challenges, conflict, and pain. Our lessons to learn. So that we may remember how to increase our energy with love, to be able to conquer a force of energy that we cannot possibly fathom. Like this is boot camp for the soul. What if..?

"Love is the highest art. In ancient times you trained so hard, not for the sake of killing people but for the love of your family: for the love of your mother, your father, your children, your tribe, and your body. It is the love of life. That's why we train so hard so you can preserve life." (Dan Inosanto)

Why should we be allowed to return *home* if we cannot unite here on Earth? Or perhaps, we are a loving species that needs to learn how to stand up for ourselves, and protect what we love, most particularly our home planet, which is currently Earth. And we need love to boost and raise the vibrational energy of consciousness to be able to shift dimensions.

Regardless of whichever version of the afterlife you choose to believe. Each and every idea implies that love and kindness will produce better results, either in this life or the next. You get what you give. In the end love does indeed conquer all.

Is it overly idealistic to think love conquers all? Well, taken into a much easier to grasp a simpler context. If you had genuine unconditional love with the people you are around on a regular basis, what would happen? What type of energy would that create within your circle? Is that energy a higher vibration or a lower vibration? The idea here is that there would be less judgment, less need for the ego to "win" in conversation with others when your starting place is love. There would be more understanding and more advancement in communication if we were making an effort to understand where a person is coming from. This understanding leads to a much higher vibrational energy of love which eventually spreads outside of your circle and across humanity. When you leave this world, what if all that mattered was love?

Singularity

Singularity is a futuristic vision that has come to fruition many times in our history through our technology. Those moments in time where there is such a *dramatic shift in human thinking* that those before the shift have difficulty comprehending the advancement. For instance, would your ancestors understand the internet? Supercomputers? Or how about all of it compacted into one small handheld device, with a camera? Amusingly, some kids today cannot comprehend life without these things.

We continue to grow our technology, creatively finding ways to make our lives *easier.* But how much are we sacrificing? People are so busy looking at their screens, failing to remember to connect to the experience and others around them in the moment. Experiences, movements, and organizations that are meant to unite humans become dividing factions of humanity. Unless we remember to connect with each other.

"For every action, there is an equal and opposite reaction." (Newton's Third Law)

It would be asinine to think that humans can continue to consume the natural resources on this planet without some repercussions from Earth. Species become extinct when their habitat has been destroyed / transformed, among other reasons. Earth is currently our habitat. The planet will balance itself out. Humans, however... have the Conscious Ability to adapt and make choices. We need to work and live WITH nature and allow nature to thrive.

"Now that we have learned to fly in the air like birds and dive in the sea like fish, only one thing remains - to learn to live on earth like humans" (George Bernard Shaw)

If we have the ability to grow and advance our technology, then we also have the Conscious Ability to advance our consciousness. Imagine singularity in humanity and consciousness. Where we see each other as brothers and sisters. Sharing our energy, wisdom, and experiences. Understanding that the energy we project affects everyone and is attracting back the same energy to ourselves. Finding the balance between the creative mind, the intuitive heart, and physical actions energy. Living Authentically.

Authentic Living means authentic giving. What are we giving to humanity as we spend time here on earth? Is it something that brings down or uplifts society? If you truly want to have more favorable experiences in your life, it would, therefore, make sense to give good energy, by your thoughts and your actions.

"Whether you believe in God or not does not matter so much, whether you believe in Buddha or not does not matter so much; as a Buddhist, whether you believe in reincarnation or not does not matter so much. You must lead a good life. And a good life does not mean just good food, good clothes, good shelter. These are not sufficient. A good motivation is what is needed: compassion, without dogmatism, without complicated philosophy; just understanding that others are human brothers and sisters and respecting their rights and human dignity." (Dalai Lama XIV)

An advanced consciousness is one of unity. Simply, bridging both your intuition and creative manifestation into one, you can start living in this advanced consciousness. Imagine taking these ideas proven by science and simplifying your lifestyle in a way that actually feels good and also makes a great impact in the world, coming from a place of unconditional love and the desire to inspire. What type of world would we have in a few years, as we practice these philosophies even just a little bit each day?

Apocalypse

"A Greek word meaning 'revelation', an unveiling or unfolding of things not previously known and which could not be known apart from the unveiling." (Wikipedia) Meaning, the apocalypse is not necessarily the complete destruction of the planet. We have the choice to advance our consciousness, by embracing the knowledge that we are discovering. We, you, I, create reality as we perceive it; combined with the attitude we have, particularly towards each other, and the actions we choose; an advancement of consciousness / humanity.

The Advancement of Humanity

The future indeed looks very bright from here. You don't have to look far to see all the problems the world encounters on a daily basis. Just turn on your television and watch the news and see how many real-world issues still face humans living on the planet today. Yet, regardless of all the problems the world faces, these are minor in comparison to what it was many decades and / or centuries ago. From here, as humanity, once we each begin to truly live by the principles we have touched on in this book, and practice coming from a place of love. Then we will advance as humanity. We see a world of prosperity, light, love, hope, and upliftment on every corner of the world, eventually.

The advancement of humanity is seen in every little good deed we do, and that is done unto us. It is in the technology space where we see more efficient ways of doing things, that is simply leading us to a better world. A world filled with humans operating both from heart and mind space and using the gifts they were all given to a higher level of humanity, an advanced level that we can all look forward to.

The advancement of humanity begins and ends with the timeless wisdom that transcends through space and time. This timeless wisdom comes in the form of unconditional love. A love without judgment, a courageous love without fear. No matter what pain you experienced in your past. Regardless of any trauma you still may be currently healing from in your current life. Without judgment on yourself and judgment of the current state of humanity, there is still hope for a bright future.

This bright future begins and ends with unconditionally loving yourself, all the mistakes you have made, no matter how big or small those mistakes or wrongs may have been. Regardless, of all the mistakes or wrongdoing others may have placed upon you. To get to the place where you can be both in the mindset and heart-space unconditionally love it all. The dark and the light of your past and even your future. Send love energy to it all, unconditionally. There can be no greater vibrational frequency than this unconditional love you have of yourself and the world around you, and that is what leads to the Authentic Self; the advancement of humanity.

Chapter 12: Utopia

We have a dream that we are sure many people share, to change the world in a positive way. We talk about it, but just how much do we do to actually make it happen? All the laws in the world only created more criminals. It is the hearts and minds of people that need to change. It can be done, provided that we each make the effort to change ourselves and how we each behave towards each other.

Do you think you cannot make a difference so why bother? Pssh! Everything you do affects the vibrations of those around you. You CAN and you ARE making a difference. Is it fear-based or love-based?

One by one, each of us has the power to make a positive change in this world. One by one, we make a positive difference. One small act of love begins a vibrational wave that has a large impact on the world. The more good vibes we create, the greater the shift to a better world, raising the vibrations of the whole planet.

How do we create these vibrational waves of positivity?

Random Acts of Kindness

An act of kindness does not have to be huge, like giving a large amount of money to a charity or buying a stranger's groceries. It can be something as simple as holding a door open for someone, cooking a meal for a neighbour, allowing a driver to merge in front of you, or listening when a friend needs to talk. It does not necessarily mean sacrificing your own wellbeing, but it does mean to give a little of yourself for the wellbeing of another; and to do it selflessly.

If you are also inclined to also do something that is considered "big," that is okay as well. Whatever it is you give out you get back. The idea here is that if you are choosing to live in a kinder world, first be kind towards others through your actions. As you get in a more habitual flow of random acts of kindness, many times it doesn't become random anymore. It becomes part of your personality. You then get into a constant flow of giving in habitual acts of kindness. You are always rewarded back in different ways from your acts of kindness that you do. Remember, your intentions are the defining line. If you are kind for the sake of a reward, your intentions are out of alignment with your heart energy and you will get exactly what you deserve,

Receiving

Many people are good at giving, but not necessarily good at receiving. The ebb and flow of life is simply this. The more you give, the more you get back. When someone offers you a gift do you accept it? When you deny a gift that someone is giving you, you are actually cutting out access to their natural ebb and flow of their giving. In order for the world to flow more harmoniously, you want to get in the flow of receiving. Receiving small gifts, or big gifts, it doesn't matter. What matters is that when you are open to the abundance of the universe. Abundance in love, material things, you are in the natural flow of all of life. Be open to receiving from the universe as well as giving. Abundance comes in many forms. Monetary abundance is not necessarily what you receive. Your perception of the world around you, paired with your attitude, will reveal your abundance. Remember to express gratitude.

What you will find is that life truly is an endless abundant place. Scarcity and lack is just a mindset. If you choose an abundant mindset then abundance comes to you. Be open to receiving abundance. You will find this world to be a rich and happy place to live.

Be the Example of Love

Love is expressed in action through kindness. For every act of love, someone witnesses or experiences this action in some way, and it becomes an inspiration for them. People will remember and mimic more of what you do, than what you say, (quantum entanglement). Children especially, learn by our actions, considerably more than what you tell them. Be the example of love for others who are learning through your behavior. As younger generations learn about love / kindness and follow or mimic the example, the greater the hope for the future of humanity becomes.

Love is at the foundation of all the best things we experience in life. Coming from a place of love in all we do, whether it is a conversation with someone, a project you take on, or a job you have; coming from love does make a huge difference in your natural flow of life, you start to attract more loving relationships and the people come in your life seem to be more loving and less judgemental. This is because you are being love, and you are attracting the energy of what you already are.

"Imagine you are walking in the woods and you see a small dog sitting by a tree. As you approach, it suddenly lunges at you, teeth bared. You are frightened and angry. But then you notice that one of its legs is caught in a trap. Immediately your mood shifts from anger to concern: You see that the dog's aggression is coming from vulnerability and pain. This applies to all of us. When we behave in hurtful ways, it is because we are caught in some kind of painful trap. The more we look through the eyes of wisdom at ourselves and each other, the more we cultivate a compassionate heart." (Tara Brach)

Accept Personal Responsibility-Accountability

The one thing you have that absolutely no one can take away from you is your Free Will. Accepting personal responsibility gives you the power to direct your life. If you make a mistake, do you cast blame on others or circumstances? Or do you accept your choices and the consequences while learning from your mistakes? You Have the Ability to choose your attitude, choose your actions, and create the life you desire. Accept it. Know it. Own it.

Every experience you need to become your authentic self has or will be there. You are not magically given strength, patience, compassion, etc. You are given opportunities to experience, learn, and choose to be. Experiences with different perspectives. The tests keep repeating until you learn the lesson, gaining wisdom with a Free Will choice to be your true Authentic Self.

Respect Nature

During this life, this is our planet, our current home. Everything we have ever done and ever will do is because the earth has supported us, providing resources for all living beings to grow and evolve; all while maintaining a balance for all life.

We can regenerate the earth and our own physical health by refusing to use chemicals that harm our soils, air, water, and us. Earth provides us with everything we need to thrive healthy. Our human physiology is designed to work WITH nature. Are you aware that weeds pull toxins out of soil to regenerate the soil? Nature is a delicate, intrinsic design for all life to thrive.

Nature is amazing when you take the time to observe and appreciate it. From the smallest ant to the largest trees. From the oceans to the deserts. Everything has a purpose, and we are part of that cycle. We are not in nature, we ARE nature. Enjoy, appreciate, and respect nature, conserving the earth for future generations.

Express Gratitude

Appreciate the little things; they make up the big things. Instead of focusing on what you do not have, focus on what you do have. What else do you have to be grateful for? A place to sleep. The clothes on your back. Every bite of food you consume... feel and express your gratitude.

Once you learn to appreciate what you have, then you begin to deserve what you want. Share this gratitude with others. When you are appreciative, those feel-good emotions vibrate out. We often hear, "I'm sorry," from others.

But just how often do we hear the words, "<u>Thank you</u>"? This phrase of gratitude has a positive impact on a person, to both the giver and the receiver. Imagine the difference of attitudes people would have with more gratitude.

Practice gratitude first thing each morning, during your day, and before you go to sleep at night. You will see that the daily, consistent regular practice of being grateful for all the good things, experiences, and people in your life begins to dramatically change your outlook on life in a very positive way, thus attracting more good things, experiences, and people in your life, because what you focus on expands.

Be a Mentor

Instead of the constant bombardment of telling someone

What not To do:	Focus on what TO do:
Don't run.	*Walk or Slow down.*
Don't scream.	*Quiet.*
Don't hit.	*Shake hands or hug.*
Don't worry.	*You can do it.*
Don't forget.	*Remember.*

Just as actions speak louder than words, the action words are where the focus and attention goes (more on this in section two).

Through focusing on what to do, you will inadvertently help those around you discover their passions, bringing out the best in them, which will also bring out the best in you.

And if nothing else, the best you can do to guide and mentor others is to be the example of love, teaching them kindness, compassion, owning up to their own actions, respect for nature, gratitude, and honesty. This will also have a more positive effect on your own attitude, health, and life.

Be the Authentic Self

To be the true you is the single most important thing you can do.

Your life experiences, the choices you make, and the attitude you have are part of shaping you mentally, emotionally, and physically. You have the choice to choose how your experiences define you. The difficult times are there to bring out your truest strengths, should you choose to work through it. When you learn to find the joy in your life, express the love in your heart, and do your best to focus on the good things, you will discover who you truly are, the authentic self. In doing so, you are the example that is giving permission for others to be themselves.

Free Will

Humans have Free Will. At the start of each day, you can choose how your day will go. You can choose to be happy, or you can choose to be unhappy. You can choose to have a successful day or choose to have an unsuccessful day. It begins with your intention. It is ultimately your decision on how things will unfold. Many will not believe this until they really start intentionally creating their reality.

When one takes part in this idea of creating a future they prefer, they are exercising their free will. This free will, when in union with the divine natural flow of life, begins to become a rather astounding force in creating a reality that brings out the authentic you, and brings about the most optimal level of growth within yourself and further enhances the utopia that is here to come on earth.

The Utopia Is Within You

There is no need to search for this utopia outside of yourself. It is already within you. Each time you are fully expressing your authentic self, being one with who you truly are. You are already in the same frequency of that utopia.

The utopia that we speak of is an internal shift, the guide that we provided here are the tools you can use. Ideas that can bring you closer to your authentic self. The utopia that is within you now is simply you are feeling good and amazing about your life. This inner state of being comes from love. To love yourself fully and to become the most authentic version of you, from that place you are more fully inclined to do good in the world and the world you perceive will change, the moment you recognize the utopia within you.

If you feel this utopia is too far-fetched, or out of reach remember, it starts with you. It begins with your thoughts and beliefs about what the world can feel and look like. Below is an affirmation you can use at the start of each day to connect. Be with oneness of you and your place on this earth.

I pledge allegiance to the Earth and all the beings who inhabit it. One world with Love. We are One. United for the highest good of all.

If any of you think that everything becomes blissful, with some magical cosmic consciousness shift without having put the work into yourself; you are mistaken. Your free will gives you the Conscious Ability and Responsibility to manage your energy.

Live

You are consciously aware of yourself, use your mind both logically and creatively. Keep learning. Have the courage to step out of your comfort zone and try new things. Accept that invitation. Make that appointment. Taste the food. Learn people's names. Make new friends. Experiment with different hobbies. Take care of your responsibilities. Go on adventures: anything outside of your comfort zone becomes an adventure with an open attitude. Experience brings growth and wisdom. Your free will gives you the Conscious Ability to be mindful of the world you create around you (perception and attitude). For as long as your consciousness resides in your present physical body. You have the opportunity to experience life as a human. Appreciate the experience.

Love

Live with passion. Love life by being mindful, respectful, and living with compassion for all beings, without judgment. Are you screaming or even thinking low vibes at the driver in front of you while you are in traffic? Or are you at peace in your mind with love in your heart, listening to your music, while you kindly allow another driver to merge? You do not have to like other people or situations, nor do you have to agree with the choices of others, but you are respectful, kind, compassionate, and feel at peace within yourself. The world is made of dreams that were created into reality by people who dared to dream with passion. Allow love to guide your free will choices, perspective, and attitude. You are not expected to hold this attitude twenty-four hours, seven days a week, but make a conscious effort. Practice becomes a habit. Habit becomes a character.

Laugh

Laughter is Joy (love) exploding into the physical. Find your joy. Appreciate the little things. When those moments arise that begin to shake you off your core... laugh. When someone does or says something and you feel the anger boiling up inside, flip that energy over with laughter; transcend the low vibes to higher vibrations. Laughter can be quite effective in most circumstances. Remember to remain respectful. Laughter, at the expense of someone's dignity or wellbeing, is impolite, and imagine the energy you would attract back...

Free Will gives you the ability to choose your reactions. Manage your reactions and choose to respond with love for yourself and with compassion for others.

Mind-Heart-Body.   Thought-Emotion-Action.
Live-Love-Laugh.   Authentic Self.

Make your life a living, thriving, moving masterpiece. Live fiercely. Love passionately. Laugh frequently. The world as we know it is ending. Crumbling under hate or thriving with love. You are left with a choice: Do you go on and continue with your ways, repeating the same vibrational energy patterns? Or do you choose to live, love, and laugh, creating a kinder, better world?

Section Two

The following pages contain advanced practice ideas for those who are open to expanding their Conscious Abilities.

What is real? What you can see? Touch? It is ALL perception. And everyone has a different perspective. Like we are all in the same house, standing in a different room, looking out different windows.

The closer you become *being and living* as your Authentic Self, you may notice more "gifts" or abilities emerging. This is not witchcraft or the "work of Satan." The human mind is quite powerful, energetically enhanced with the heart energy, especially with love.

Supernatural or Natural?

Everyone is capable of reaching a higher consciousness. Everyone is capable of tapping into their most innate abilities that we perceive as psychic or gifted. Just as some people have a more natural ability to run like the wind, calculate complex mathematical equations in their head, or compose a symphony, there are some who have a natural intuitive ability.

Whether you have gut feelings (intuition) or psychic visions, empathic senses, aura reading, telepathy, telekinesis, astral projection, clairsentience, clairvoyance, clairaudience, psychometry, channelling, remote viewing, or many other "supernatural" abilities; you should remember that these are NOT supernatural. Nor do these abilities work separately. The abilities are a natural part of you, a natural human ability.

In many humans, those abilities are remaining unused. It is scientifically proven that the average human being uses only a small percentage of their brain wiring. What if the rest is what enables us all to use those psychic abilities if they are activated?

Children today are growing up in a society that is more accepting of these abilities, so these younger generations are less likely to forget them and are actually able to fine tune their skills.

This Is Only the Beginning

Intention is the defining line. It is a fine balance between humility and arrogance. It is a matter of absolutely believing in yourself without boasting about yourself or getting too attached to one certain outcome of how what you desire manifests. Your intentions will determine the direction your energy flows. How you identify yourself, recognize your abilities, and how you use your abilities in the world will create your path.

Identity

The human language, regions and beliefs have created so many different labels to define us. Between nationality, race, gender - identity, sexual preference, generations, politics, religions, zodiacs, professions and level of consciousness, the human race has divided. Do you allow the label to define you or do you define the label? The only "label" that is truly yours is your own name; the rest are simply ideas.

The previous mentioned are just labels, humans like labels. It is the label that brings you to others with similar ideas and beliefs. No one is less than or better than others just because they are aware of things others are not or have different interests and beliefs. We are all the same with the same potential. We all have free will as to how much we open ourselves up to new levels of consciousness. Everyone has the capability of connecting with the higher self, as long as they are paying attention.

Let go of the labels and simply be your true Authentic Self. To find your true self at the core of your soul, match your thoughts and emotions with your actions, expressed with love, kindness, and compassion.

Encourage your children to be themselves. Encourage them to embrace their inner strengths and abilities. Encourage them (period). Not an easy thing to do in a society that tries to put everyone in a box. You, and everyone else, is far more capable of achieving things than the limitations you have been taught to believe. We encourage you to believe in yourself.

As far as manifesting things... this is the Law of Attraction (LOA). You get what you focus on, what dominates your thoughts. LOA does not recognize positives and negatives, only the main point of focus. This is also how karma works, along with prayer, the golden rule, and quantum physics, same concept, different labels.

Do you think your path is already written? You determine your destiny. Your whole life, with all of your experiences that you attracted to yourself to learn, is weaving together to create the destiny that you are focused on, your own set goals. Anything outside of your own consciousness is an extension of you, your own creation of your perception.

Helping Humanity

Now that you are discovering these abilities within you, and most likely you are still discovering the unlimited capabilities, what are you doing with your life? How are you affecting those around you? Is it helpful? Is it kind?

"I am only one, but still, I am one. I cannot do everything, but still, I can do something; and because I cannot do everything, I will not refuse to do something that I can do." (Helen Keller)

Some people are likely to open up to you and tell you their life story because they just sense you are a good listener and helper by nature. Let them talk, tell their story and try as best you can to stay present with compassion and without judgment. Remember, you can be a guidepost and point the direction of change if you feel they are on the wrong path, but you cannot drag them along the right one. Understand the difference between compassion and enabling. Sometimes the other person has to walk their path alone. Comforting someone is a kind thing to do. Encouraging them to believe in their own strength has a longer lasting effect. You can only help those who are willing to help themselves.

Be the Master of You

When you learn to appreciate what you have, then you will begin to deserve more. This life is yours. Every thought you have, every intention you set, every emotion you feel, every action you take (mind, spirit and body) determines which direction you choose to focus your own life path.

Know when to take some time to retreat and go within to release, relax, rejuvenate, and heal to make room for a fresh new positive outlook on life.

Trust your senses, let go of the labels and be your true authentic self, in ALL aspects of your life. Own up to your responsibilities and develop your character with integrity. Be love with kindness and compassion for all beings. Hold an attitude of gratitude and you will discover and walk YOUR path.

You are a unique piece of the universal consciousness. Your authenticity is appreciated.

Chapter 13: How Language Shapes Your Reality

"Words cast spells that's why it's called SPELLING"
(unknown) There so much truth in this statement and yet, the majority of the popular inspirational quotes, as well as self-help tips, books, and even the ancient religious Ten Commandments, all have a negative connotation.

You may be gasping by now, at the very thought that we referred to inspiration and the Ten Commandments to be negative. The choice of words used directs the focus and presents the vibes of the message. When you focus on what not to do, even though you are saying, "Don't," you are in fact, giving attention to the very act of what has been said not to do.

For those times you do feel the need to express a negative choice, it can still be presented in a positive way. A simple example: "Don't touch. Wet paint." Which of course, focuses on "touch" and let's be honest, how many people still go ahead and touch the paint? What could be said instead, "Careful. Wet paint." This informs the person of the wet paint and focuses on being careful.

Here are 3 popular, inspirational memes that have circulated the internet. The words are actually focusing on the negative, yet they are masked as positive. We have rewritten and recreated each one with a new and positive version of each.

Positivity Pledge:

(original)

I shall no longer <u>allow</u> <u>negative</u>
thoughts or feelings
to <u>drain</u> <u>me</u> of my energy.
Instead, I shall focus on all the
good that is in my life.
I will think it, feel it, and speak it.
By doing so I will send out
vibes of positive energy
into the world and I <u>shall</u> be
grateful for all the wonderful things it <u>will</u> attract into my life.

(rewrite)

I <u>am</u> focusing
on all the good that
is in my life. I <u>am</u> thinking,
feeling, and speaking good.
I <u>am</u> sending out vibes of
positive energy into the
world and I <u>am</u> grateful
for all the wonderful
things I attract into my life.

Many would find this inspirational, but do you see negativity? Our brains have been conditioned to speak this way. When you consciously choose your words, you can rewrite your attitude and your life. Do you see the difference? Instead of focusing on what not to do, redirect your words and thoughts and focus on what To Do. How about another one?

This next one is full of "don'ts" and "never's" True, it is some good advice. What if this was written in a slightly more positive way?

12 steps for self-care:

1. If it feels <u>wrong,</u> don't <u>do it</u>
2. Say exactly what you mean
3. Don't <u>be</u> a <u>people pleaser</u>
4. Trust your instinct
5. Never <u>speak bad</u> about yourself
6. Never <u>give up</u> on your dreams
7. Don't <u>be afraid</u> to say no
8. Don't <u>be afraid</u> to say yes
9. Be kind to yourself
10. Let go of what you can't control
11. <u>Stay</u> away from <u>drama</u> and <u>negativity</u>
12. LOVE

The Rewrite:

1. If it feels wrong, <u>walk away</u> from it.
2. Say "exactly" what you mean.
3. Trust your instincts.
4. <u>Speak good</u> to yourself.
5. <u>Have</u> the <u>courage</u> to say, "No."
6. <u>Have</u> the <u>courage</u> to say, "Yes."
7. <u>Go after</u> and grab hold of your dreams.
8. <u>Laugh</u> at the little things.
9. Be KIND to yourself.
10. <u>Forgive</u> yourself.
11. <u>Look</u> for the <u>positive</u> and <u>beauty</u> in things.
12. LOVE

Can you feel the difference in the vibes of the words? Which one compels you more? Which of these direct your mind to focus on the positive viewpoint? This next one is quite a popular prayer. But wait. Would you constantly tell someone they are bad or broken and need to be saved? This is narcissistic behavior. Followed by our rewrite.

Enlighten what's dark in me   *Strengthen Me*

Mend what's broken in me   *I Am Enlightening.*
Bind what's bruised in me   *I Am Strengthening.*
Heal what's sick in me   *I Am Mending.*
and lastly,   *I Am Repairing.*
Revive whatever peace and   *I Am Healing.*
love has died in me   *I Am Reviving the*
          Peace and Love within Me

Encouragement and focusing on the good, will bring out more goodness in yourself, as well as others. "I Am" is an affirmation. Remember, the words you choose have the power to reshape your perspective and reality. You can call this the Law of Attraction, or simply understand it is a basic language tool.

The words you choose to tell yourself, and the emotions attached to those words, becomes your perspective and belief about yourself. Make a conscious effort to change your choice of words, directing your focus to the positive. Give your attention to what you desire and wish to manifest into your reality.

It Starts with a Thought

Here is where you have to really get the words / image right along with the heart. If you think "I need..." you will always need it. If you think "I want..." you will continue to want. If you think "I have..." then you will have. It is already here in the present moment. It is all in the phrasing, the LOA is very literal. Remember, you are attracting back the same energy you put out.

Attitude Makes A Difference

People today generally are quick to complain about situations or a person they may be dealing with. It has almost become a default setting to focus on the negative. When you hear others say to "focus on the positive" they are not kidding. You are going to get what you deserve, so check your emotions. Even people will be what you think them to be. If you call someone an idiot, then to you that is just what they will be. By calling someone smart or thoughtful, then you have given them the opportunity to rise up to that. With a positive attitude, you attract positive things.

The Positive Mind Wins

Thinking in terms of winning and losing. Compared to a negative thinker, we can make the argument that the positive thinker wins at the end of the day. Why is this? An example would be our health.

When your body is unhealthy it is not a good feeling. When your body is feeling healthy it is a good feeling. Same with life events and circumstances. Do we wake up wanting to have a bad day? No. Generally, we desire to have the best possible day. If we continually come to each day from a place of gratitude.

Feeling the feelings of what already is going well in our life if we start from there. We can start to enhance and practice with a more positive mindset, that wins. A well-developed positive thinking mindset wins at the start of the day, during the day, and when you go to sleep at night. Even while you are sleeping the subconscious mind that takes over becomes more positive, you have nicer and better dreams because of the thoughts you are thinking in your day-to-day.

Positive thinking comes naturally to others, while some may struggle with this. A lot of this struggle comes from early childhood conditioning that you are not good enough. Or you are not smart or beautiful enough. The reality is you can reprogram that through practicing being gentler with your childhood beliefs. Turning the limiting beliefs into more empowering, positive beliefs that change your future for the better. Practice using positive words in conversation with others. Words have power. Whatever you say in conversation with others, is prophesying your future. What we continually consciously or unconsciously say to ourselves in quiet or out loud are also self-fulfilling prophecies.

The idea here is you want to practice positive thinking daily. Whenever you slip into the negative, it takes mental discipline to reframe it back into the positive. It is a challenge you can commit to each day, being aware of which thoughts you think bring you to the negative, and which bring you to the positive.

If you ever doubted the power of positive thinking, that doubt in and of itself is already a negative limited belief, that once again you were programmed to believe is true from your childhood. This is why a lot of this practice is not just a one-time fix, rather a way of life. A daily discipline.

The positive mind will win because it comes from a place of love. Love infused with positive energy in taking action necessary to win, it will put you in a position to further enhance the quality of your life while maintaining the entry of your true authentic self. Taking action from this space with a positive mindset, constantly using words that enhance your life brings about everlasting joy and happiness that is real and can be felt by others around you.

Taking Action

Are you one of those people that wishes they would win the lottery but never buy a ticket? You have to go after your dreams. Talk to people. Grab hold of opportunities when presented to you. With the right attitude, you can make things happen. Absolute belief is the key.

Practicing the right attitude and putting it to action is the challenge. First of all, think IN the positive and present tense. If you believe it will not work, then you are correct that it will not work. But in that sense, it does work for the simple fact you believe it does not work that is what works. (Have fun wrapping your mind around that one). But by genuinely believing, balance your Karma, live in the moment, and a positive attitude anything is possible.

Chapter 14: Empathy 101

Have you ever felt sad, angry, or happy and could not think of an obvious reason within your experience why you feel that way? Have you been in someone's presence and could feel their physical and/or emotional pain within you? Congratulations, you have experienced empathy. We have already explained the heart's electromagnetic field in chapter four. Your awareness unlocks Empathy.

Recognizing Your Empathic Ability

Most people who are aware of their empathic abilities often express their frustration, "*Ugh! I can't take it! I can't stand being around all this negative energy from everyone. I've had it!*" Hold on now. Do you realize that right there you are sending out and also attracting more negative energy?

Every thought you think, every word you say, every emotion you feel and every action you take is energy. That energy goes out to others and has a direct effect on the world around you. This is not philosophy, this is science. You have it within you the Conscious Ability to transform emotional energy into a positive state. It all begins from within, your own attitude and perspective.

Managing Your Empathy Skills

First and foremost, you must be able to recognize and manage your own emotions. You cannot shut down your emotions, you only ignore them. What happens when an animal in a cage that has been ignored and it gets out? You feel something. Recognize it. Know it. Own it. Manage it.

In any situation you find yourself, possibly feeling an overload of emotions, first ask yourself, "Do these feelings belong to me?" If the answer is, "No, these feelings are not mine," wrap them up in love and "return to sender." Knowing yourself, being your Authentic Self, is key to being able to recognize your own feelings or emotions separately from others. If the answer is yes, those are yours, allow yourself to be present with what is there and also surround those negative energies with loving energy, perhaps breathing into it and releasing what no longer serves you, transforming it.

"I once walked into my parents' home and within two minutes I was feeling angry. I paused for a moment, realizing that I was not angry, but I was sensing the energy in the home. I wrapped up those emotions with love and returned them. I also planted my feet, grounding myself and consciously sent out positive energy through the house. I honestly cannot say if it changed the sender's mood (I like to believe it did), but those negative energies no longer affected my mood." (Deidra Rae)

Once you can recognize and manage your own emotions, including your outward reaction to situations, you can learn to master your empathic ability. It starts with creating a "shield" or an energy bubble (for lack of a better term). The armour of light energy shield you surround yourself with like a bubble that cannot be physically seen, only felt. It is your "personal space" that only those you allow to penetrate can get through. Think of it as a filter. You choose what you allow to affect you.

Creating the "Shield"

Calm your mind and center yourself. Inhale through your nose and exhale through your mouth; taking long deep breaths. Much like what you would do in meditation. You can do this with your eyes open or closed, whichever you are most comfortable with. See the light within you, that glow of energy that is the essence of your soul and push that light outward. Surround yourself with your light energy. Or visualize your electromagnetic field. It is already extended beyond your body, consciously use the heart's energy field... You can make the shield as thick as you would like it. After doing this, pay attention to how you are feeling. I bet you are already feeling calmer and more relaxed.

Try using this shielding technique before you enter a gathering of people, events, or any public areas where there are a lot of people and activities taking place. This shielding technique works especially well in crowded places.

The shield serves as a conscious reminder to filter and manage what you feel from others. It does not have to be a "full shield" or "no shield." You can extend your shield out to others like reaching your hand out to touch them; all it takes is the thought. You can receive emotions as well as send out emotions. Be careful what kind you send out; you certainly do not want to create more negativity. Here are some practice exercises to help you learn how to manage empathy.

**NOTE: You can choose who you connect with. You are not invading their privacy. If they do not want to be felt, they will be shielded (consciously or subconsciously). We each feel others' emotions without realizing it. With these conscious practices, you awaken your awareness, and you can learn to manage what you feel and how to recognize where the emotions are coming from, along with sending out.

Practicing with Empathy Skills

Practice Exercise #1 — One on One Connection
1. Center yourself, calm your mind and create your energy bubble.

2. Choose one person and extend that energy field you created out to them. Feel that one person's emotions. Pull your energy field back closer to your body

3. Extend your energy field back out to that person and send them a "virtual hug," positive vibrations. And watch the expression on their face.

4. Pull your energy bubble back closer to you and choose another person.

Practice Exercise #2 — Spaces and Places

1. Center yourself, calm your mind and create your energy bubble.

2. Walk into a public place. Push your energetic field / shield outward. Fill the place with positive vibes.

3. Put a second shield up around you by finding the light within you and push it outward, keeping it close to your body.

4. Anyone who is giving off negative energies or vibrations, put another shield around them with mirrors inside towards that person; their negativity will reflect back to them.

Practice Exercise #3 — Sensing Surrounding Energies
1. Center yourself, calm your mind and shield up.

2. Stand still and focus on energies in front of you. What do you feel? Sense?

3. Focus on energies to the right. To the left. Behind you. Focus on one area at a time.

4. Practice clockwise, counter clockwise, and random directions.

Go out, practice and experiment with your discovered ability. Keeping your heart and mind in a place of joy and love will strengthen your shield as well as affect others with your positive energy.

Using Empathy in Your Daily Life

If you realize you have the empathic skills, which we believe everyone has the capability, then you can consciously help others and raise the vibes on the planet. When you go out into public, you can make a mental effort to send out good vibes. Walk around smiling, giggling, and humming under your breath, as you feel your energies spread out. By the way, smiling, laughing, singing, and dancing are a few things you can do to raise your own vibes. You can help make a difference just by keeping your own positive energy up and help to raise others.

Here is an example of what you can do with your own empathic skills:

"One night we (my Love and I) went out to dinner. Near the end of our meal, I was overwhelmed with emotions with a part of me that wanted to cry. I realized it was not me. I was fine; it was someone or more than one person in the restaurant. At first, I looked around, connecting with different individuals, feeling their emotions. But then I decided to just "send it out" and fill the room with good vibes. I sat there quietly humming a little tune, pushing out "happy vibes" in all directions around me. My Love touched my hand and asked me if I was ok because I was so quiet. "I'm working," I told him. With him holding my hand, it was a boost of energy and I was able to send out more. When we got up to leave, I walked past one of the waitresses sensing that she was the one who wanted to cry. I wrapped her up in a 'virtual hug'." (Deidra Rae)

Everything you do is energy. How are you affecting the world? Is it positive? Is it kind? Your attitude is YOUR CHOICE. You are the manager of your thoughts, emotions, and actions. What you think, say, feel and do in your everyday life is where you can truly make a difference.

Sensing Energies of Objects or Spaces

An imprint of energy is what remains long after a person has walked away, or an event has taken place. Feeling an imprint of energy on an object by touching it or being in close proximity is called psychometry, in many ways, an extension of empathy. You may feel the energy of the owner of the object or possibly even layers of energy from others who have touched it. As your abilities and awareness grow, you may even "see" the history in your mind.

Sensing the imprint of energies in a space is also quite common. Have you ever walked into a room and felt strange? Almost as if you "know" what happened in that space recently. You can also send loving light to these objects or into a space, transforming any negative energy into positive.

Empathy over Distances

Empathic energies are not limited in great distances. In fact, energy can travel at any distance in only a moment's time. With the rise of communications via phone calls, text messages and social networks over the internet, we have the ability to connect with people around the world. This connection gives us optimal ways to understand others on so many levels.

Have you heard of the phrase, "Reading between the lines"? This is true in a very literal sense. Not only can you hear or read a person's words, but you can also feel the energy behind their words. **If you would like a little practice with "reading between the lines" this book you are reading at this very moment is written by two co-authors. Can you tell the difference in the writing? Do you feel the different energies pertaining to different sections and chapters? It is ok if you do not. We honestly hope we blended our writing well together.

Reading words or listening to a voice speak is one way to connect empathically. It is very possible to connect with someone at an emotional or physical level, even from across the planet. To do this, focus on the person and pay attention to what you feel.

Most people will not believe that this is possible. Many will deny it. You do not need their belief so long as you believe it can be done. If your idea of having certain abilities is to show off to others, you are missing the point. You have the ability to truly understand and help others; to truly make a positive difference in the world.

"To selflessly make a positive difference in someone's life, is the most amazing gift you can give of yourself." (Deidra Rae)

Chapter 15: Jesus Christ

The elephant in the room, well this is great but what about religion? Where does religion play into all of this? Let us talk about Jesus and let's talk about the teachings of Jesus, and why at the core of His teachings we find truth.

A lot of what is written here is just an experience, not based on religious dogma. So, follow along as much as possible, so you can come to your own conclusions. There is a light in the world, and that light in the world may very well be in the teachings of Jesus when Jesus had this to say while debating with the Jews: *"I am the light of the world. Whoever follows me will never walk in darkness but will have the light of life." (John 8:12)*

Whether or not people want to take that literally or not, it is a pretty bold statement. In the previous chapters we spoke about the I AM in the form of affirmations. Yet, this text in the Bible has been passed on for many centuries therefore the repetition of people reading this text made it real. You see, what we repeatedly read and gets passed down becomes a reality.

Aside from all the religious talk, there is A Christ Consciousness. A feeling you get when you reach out to Jesus. This is because if you call on Jesus, he will come to you (the belief is what makes it real). Much like using a tool to focus on. Calling upon Jesus for assistance is making you consciously aware of your focus and believe in yourself. The Bible can be interpreted in many different ways.

Yet at the same time, you already have read in this book so far, some teachings inspired by Jesus. Many teachings of Jesus are universal and can be applied in everyday life regardless of what your religious or non-religious beliefs may be. Many of Jesus' teachings are timeless. Which are also quite similar to Buddha's teachings. Practicing the wisdom, you will find a sense of "knowing" Jesus at a level that goes beyond the religious dogmas and the division and separation that takes place with most religions. To say one is right or wrong about their experience of Jesus is already causing further division, at a time when the earth needs more oneness and mutual understanding. The message in Jesus' teachings is to love. Love is the primary message Jesus taught his disciples.

"People do not need Jesus. People need to BE like Jesus. With love, kindness and compassion." (Anonymous)

Imagine a world where the teachings of Jesus improved the world instead of causing division. Imagine a world where we did not have to say what religion we were to know Jesus and practice the wisdom he taught that greatly improved and advanced our consciousness into love, peace and harmony with each other and greater respect and understanding for all people on this planet.

Some of you are probably annoyed at the mere mention of Jesus. The man existed. As the son of God is debatable. But what he taught to the people was to believe in something greater than what they were able to understand. He encouraged kindness and compassion for all beings, without judgment.

The Golden Rule: Do unto Others What You Want Done unto You

"So, in everything, do to others what you would have them do to you." (Matthew 7:12)

"All tremble at punishment. Life is dear to all. Put yourself in the place of others and harm none nor have them harmed." (Buddha)

Practicing one of the core teachings of Jesus, do unto others what we want done unto us can indeed work wonders in the life of others and even for one's own life. The reason is that what we give out we get back. Before deciding to take any major action towards someone. Ask yourself this simple question, "Would I want someone to do this exact action unto me?" If then the answer is yes, then continue forward. If the answer is no, then maybe reconsider your intent.

"Give, and it will be given to you. A good measure, pressed down, shaken together, and running over, will be poured into your lap. For with the measure you use, it will be measured to you." (Luke 6:38)

We can never fully get this perfect but being conscious of this teaching can in fact overtime make this world a better place. Imagine a world where every conscious and evolved human was doing unto others what they want done unto them. The joy, love, and peace would be abundant all across the entire earth we live in.

Confession

If, and when (you are human), you infringe on someone's human rights, cause harm, or any discord towards another being, be accountable and rectify the energy you created to the best of your capabilities. Confessing in prayer or to a priest only passes that energy you created on to others. Instead, confess to the person you've wronged and make it right.

Confessing is all about taking personal responsibility. Having the level of awareness to know when you may have caused harm to another person and confessing that you made a mistake and learning from it, shows that your soul is growing and evolving. Confessing is about self-awareness as well. When you confess the person about the harm you caused, you are becoming more self-aware in the process, because you are becoming more conscious about your next actions you take, hopefully not repeating the same mistakes again.

There is a liberating feeling when you confess any harm you may have caused another person. By confessing said harm you may have caused another person, you free up the stagnant negative energy when you release it. Creating a clearer and positive energy around you. The opposite is also true. When you forgive others for the harm, they have caused you, you are also liberated. The energy is cleared, and you actually start to feel lighter, more able to move around the world in a more relaxed, healthy, and less judgemental space.

God

This has nothing to do with believing in God. Religions are one of the main causes of wars. Humans are so focused on claiming which religion is right, they forget the purpose of believing. Believe there is something greater. The light in the world is within each of you. The light is Love, pure energy.

"God is consciousness... not a creator. God is the source of creation itself. It (not he or she) IT is not independent of you. It is the totality of everything. So, when I call myself God I am not talking about the expression of the God-self that rests inside of me. The verb... the ENERGY... not the noun. Once you think God is a noun, person, place, or thing, you separate yourself from it and immediately become a limited being. That's what separates the believers (religious) from the knowers (spiritual)." (Unknown)

Whether you call "IT" God, Source, or Consciousness, "IT" is pure energy, from which all is connected. "God" is an identity humans gave to something that does not have an identity. The definition of a god is an external, supernatural deity. So as "God" is not external from you, but rather your internal conscious, the pure energy, which is the core of your being, then logically, "God" is not a god.

Even Jesus said, *"The kingdom of God is within you." (Luke 17:21)* On a higher level of consciousness, we are all connected. You have free will because your thoughts, from your conscious, are the creator of your reality. And you alone are responsible for your thoughts. This is how prayer works. This is how karma works. This is how the Law of Attraction works. Same concept with different labels.

When it is said, "God is love," that is literal! The love within each of you, your natural state of being, the pure energy of your soul, is the driving force of energy creating this world. It is expressed through our actions, kindness, and compassion. Feed THAT energy. UNITE under one race, the Human race.

Just a side note: A benevolent God would never demand the people to kill in his name. The god would dismantle the "sinners" themselves instead of demanding the people to commit a sin.

Once you let go of the idea of a god-being controlling your life, accepting that your reality is shaped and experienced through your thoughts, emotions, and physical actions.
        (father-holy spirit-son = mind-heart-body),
You allow yourself to consciously create and direct your life. Remember, you have Free Will.

Religions work the way they were intended to work, control the masses by keeping them in fear. If religions worked the way the masses think is the purpose, the world would not be in the state of turmoil that it is in today. The greatest trick ever played was to have us search externally for a saviour when we are here to save ourselves.

The more people wake up, expand their minds out of the box of dogma, realizing that all things are energy and begin with a conscious thought, take responsibility for their own thoughts, emotions, and actions, guide the new generations with love, kindness and compassion, leaving behind fear, hate and judgement, then just maybe, we can create an undivided world.

Chapter 16: Intuition

You have chosen to continue reading. Are you ready for more? Have you ever had a "gut feeling?" Have you ever been in a situation where something just did not feel right? Or have you ever felt so sure of something, but you are unable to explain how you know?

To put a label on this knowing... *"Intuition is the ability to understand something immediately, without the need for conscious reasoning." (Dictionary)* This can be simply explained, however, the *"feeling"* of intuition may be different for everyone.

The human body produces chemicals to act as neurotransmitters, responsible for sending messages from neuron to neuron throughout the body. Physiologically, the brain communicates to the body through nerves, relaying messages to neurons. Dopamine, Serotonin, Oxytocin, and Endorphins are the four neurotransmitter chemicals that are responsible for happiness because they induce those "feel good" emotions and physical wellness.

Amazingly, you can help trigger your body to produce more of these happy chemicals. Specific foods (do your own research), exercise, and acts of kindness... Yes, you read that correctly. Acts of Kindness, giving as well as receiving, increases your happy chemicals.

Serotonin, one of the four happy chemicals, is mainly produced in the gastrointestinal (GI) tract, however, some are found in the brain stem. The GI tract also called the enteric nervous system (ENS) is sometimes called the *second brain* because it operates independently from your main brain - the central nervous system (CNS). However, your brain and gut communicate via the vagus nerve, using serotonin to transmit the messages. Very simply, the vagus nerve transmits messages between the brain, heart, lungs, and GI tract. When the vagus nerve is stimulated, it helps you make memories with some memories becoming INSTINCTIVE.

Are you following?... Subconsciously you pick up subtle clues of surrounding energies and patterns through your senses. Your cells and brains store memories of these subtle clues. Subconsciously, you are organizing these memories, so that when the same or similar energy patterns arise, you subconsciously alert yourself.

Your body is communicating with your heart and mind through your gut. And when you learn to trust that "*gut feeling*" you are listening to your intuition. Basically, the more you exercise, eat healthily, and partake in acts of kindness (giving and receiving); your body will create more happy chemicals, raising your vibrations and increasing the connection between the trinity of your mind-heart-body. The intuitive *feeling* is unexplainable. It may be different for everyone, but you will KNOW your intuition when it awakens. [*This is neither complete nor exact, this is an interpretation / perspective.*]

Intuition and Trust

The more you trust this process of following your intuition, the stronger your intuitive ability gets over time. We use the example of going to the gym for the first time. When you first decide to lift weights, to build your muscles, and you have not done so your whole life, it is difficult to lift the weights to develop your muscles. It feels like a struggle at first, for you to trust that the act of lifting weights is actually doing anything at all (in this example).

Yet, you persist, knowing that you will eventually see results; the more you practice and lift the weights. You know, by gradually exercising the muscles regularly, the stronger your muscles become. Over a period of time, you feel stronger and you also see physical results.

The same is true when you start attempting to develop your intuition. At first, it may seem like nothing is "happening" or you are not seeing "results." It may even at first feel like you are overthinking the situation, and it is hard to trust something that you have never really been told to practice. However, the more you exercise your intuition and begin to trust your intuition the stronger and more developed your intuition gets over a period of time. As you practice using it you start to trust your intuition until your confidence in it grows and you become a master of your intuition, thus a master of yourself.

You know. That pit-in-your-stomach feeling that alerts you to pay attention to what you are sensing? It is not always a warning. It could be a signal to move forward with your project. Most often it is a warning. Other neurotransmitters are responsible for your *fight-or-flight* response: dopamine, epinephrine (adrenaline) and norepinephrine (noradrenaline), which are released during the body's stress response. Your body is designed to protect itself.

Following are real-life stories of when people have trusted their intuition, told from the perspective of the narrator.

"I was driving home from work, late one evening. I stopped at an intersection to turn left. I was stopped in a position where I could not see the cross traffic before they reached the intersection; a large metal electrical box was impeding my view. My traffic light turned green and my gut told me to wait. That moment, a large work truck blew through his traffic light, which was red for the cross traffic. Had I not listened to my intuition; I would have surely been hit by this truck... Maybe I subconsciously felt the truck coming." (Deidra Rae)

"My daughter Elizabeth was about 4 years old, and I was looking for a new day-care for her. I looked in the Anaheim yellow pages (1996!), and found one nearby, I drove over to check it out. It turned out to be at what looked like a big apartment complex. As I pulled into the parking lot, I saw that beyond the gate was a swimming pool. Suddenly I was filled with dread. A dark, dark cloud came over me. My mind screamed NOPE. I tried to rationalize with myself. But my hand-scribbled out the name in the phone book until I could not read the name and number anymore. I was mad at myself and felt foolish, but I decided to trust this strange dark feeling. I drove home. I walked in the door and saw the answering machine had missed calls and messages. I pushed play and it was my Mom, calling from northern California. ALL of the calls were from my Mom. She said, "Laura, call me right now!!!" I dialed her number and she immediately asked, "Where is Elizabeth? Is she ok?"

I told her she was still at the babysitter's. Mom said frantically, "Please go get her. Please call over there right now and make sure she is ok. I just have this strong feeling that she is floating in a pool!!!!" Freaking out, I called the babysitter, who did have an above ground pool. She assured me that the gate was locked, and Elizabeth was fine. I drove straight over to pick her up. When I got home my Mom called again. She said that Dad had just called her from work, which he never does. He told her, "Paula, I just can't shake this bad dream I had last night. I dreamed a little girl was floating face down in the water. Can you call Laura because I think it was Elizabeth in my dream." I cried and cried when Mom told me this, and I'm crying now as I retell the story. I assured her that I had Elizabeth with me. I still don't know how to explain this, without using words like connection, intuition, guardian angels, or magic. And to wonder how it could be that I had the strong feeling of Don't, at the same time as my Mom who was hundreds of miles away, and that my Dad had had the premonition the night before." (Laura Hoyle)

"Before we moved, we (my siblings and I) were in our shared bedroom, playing Barbies or something when the meanest uncle opened our door all of sudden and in a loud and scary way. We were all afraid of course, being little kids. He was there yelling at us, asking who left the light on in the basement. It was none of us since we knew to always clean up after ourselves and turn off anything so that we wouldn't get in trouble. We had a slightly autistic cousin who was actually Aunt 'M's' son who always plays video games in the basement. It was actually him who left the lights on, but since he was the only male son in our extended family, and since he was my aunt's son, he never got in trouble.

The mean uncle actually said, "Well someone has to turn the lights off." I knew that if we all kept quiet, we would all get the punishment. So, I took one for the team and said, "I will turn them off, thinking to just get it over with. So, downstairs I went with him following behind me. It was a very tense time just going all the way downstairs with the heat of his angry stare behind my head.

I turned off the lights, then went up the basement stairs. By the time I got to the second set of stairs to get to the kitchen, something told me to turn around and put my arm up to cover my face. I did not hesitate and when I did, sure enough, he was waiting for me with a vacuum attachment and in mid-strike. I blocked him, but I knew that if I did that, it would mean that I was defying him. So, I put my arm down and fell back onto the stair steps where he took satisfaction in hitting me with said vacuum attachment. I was shaken but didn't feel pain because I was in shock." (Anonymous)

As you are processing what you have read, here. Take a moment to listen to your intuition.
We will wait.

…

…

…

…

…

…

…

…

…

…

…

…

Does this resonate with you? Meaning, do you feel the motivation to understand more?

If you have no other ability to work for you, you have your intuition. That sense of knowing without having all the information or knowing that there is still something hidden. You may not be able to explain it entirely, but you feel it.

Clairsentience is almost the same as intuition, just a little more fine-tuned. As your awareness increases, so does this sense of knowing. For some, it may be an energetic pull when facing a choice of direction. It could be ringing in the ears or goosebumps on the skin. It could be your heart beating just a little bit faster. These are some of the physical signs, which sometimes accompany this sense, but not always.

Chapter 17: Visions

Remember those neurotransmitters? And cells storing memories? We all dream, and we certainly think using images. The popular use of emojis when humans communicate accurately shows the commonality of using images as a language. As your body picks up subtle clues of surrounding energies, storing, and organizing these memories, your subconscious mind reveals to you that it has pieced together, through visions. When you sleep, visions come in the form of dreams, most often what has been occupying your mind. When you are awake, visions may just pop into your head at random moments. Have you ever had an image come to your mind, and you are questioning why you thought of this image?

The media had portrayed a misconception about what it is like to receive a vision. The dramatization is for entertainment purposes. Yes, there are frauds out there. But there are also many humans who legitimately are able to "see" and decipher the visions they receive. Again, your mind, working with your entire body, is organizing all of the information it has collected. And when you need it, your subconscious will SHOUT at you, in a way that gets your attention. Sometimes that shout is an image or a mini movie playing in your mind.

Some people have the ability to see clearly in pictures into the future, through visions. Clairvoyance (from French Clair meaning "clear" and Voyance meaning "vision") is the ability to gain information about a person, object, location, or physical event through extrasensory perception. The subconscious mind has predicted possibilities of what is to come, based on the energy patterns it has been storing. Keep in mind, however, that not all visions are 100% accurate. Some are just images you are imagining over and over in your mind, based on the thoughts you are choosing to think. Or even thoughts / beliefs that your mom or dad, teachers, television programs, etc, repeated over and over to you early in your childhood (programming). But this is where it gets interesting. The thoughts you focus on are the energies you are attracting to you, joined with the actions you choose to take. In some form, the vision is manifested into reality, simply by focusing on it.

Visions can be broken up into categories for the beginner or for someone who is becoming aware. With practice, experience, and increased awareness, you may come to realize that the different types of visions overlap, blend together, and work with other abilities. The labels help describe the possibilities, yet this is beyond language. This is Energy.

Premonition and Precognition – Future Sight

One misconceived notion about future sight is that it is certain; and when the events fail to match a future vision, it is thought the psychic is a fraud. The future is NOT set. There are many variables (everyone's free will) that can redirect the outcome. Any future type of vision is only one of many possibilities.

What this type of sight can provide is direction. Your inner soul subconscious may show you anything from a glimpse to a full played out movie in your mind of what could be. The subconscious mind has already mapped out possible futures. The conscious mind recognizes pieces through visions / premonitions or precognitions. When you connect the conscious with the subconscious by being authentic and know that you create the future you focus on, you have the ability to change the vision.

At the time of getting the vision, there is certain energy attached to that vision from the time and space that you are currently in. Therefore, that vision you have the future can change depending on your free will with your thoughts and actions. It can also change based on the free will, thoughts, and actions of others. There are also visions that may actually become reality faster than others while some take a much longer amount of time to come into physical reality. Regardless, of the time it takes the vision, it is a part of a peak of what may be a potential future. It still really is up to You how it ends.

For example, let us say you have a vision, or a dream, one day of becoming a famous singer. In this vision you see a vision of crowds of fans swarming you after a concert you put on. People love your music, and you see another vision of your music being played in night clubs and on smartphones across the globe. This vision may have come to you very clearly, however, if you never bother to take time out of your day to actually sit down on a chair, take out your tablet or device and write a single song, or hit the record button on a single song you sing...

That vision of you becoming a famous singer may never really come to pass in physical reality. The vision still must come with you aligning to the vision and taking the action steps, having the right mindset, and drive to carry it through. (It is time to write that song.)

The accuracy of a vision is directly correlated to the actionable steps, and thoughts prior to the vision taking place in physical reality.

To enhance this ability, and to apply the Law of Attraction (LOA), practice visualization.

- Live authentically and mindfully.

- When you are beginning a project, see the progress and end result.

- Any worry may cause undesired results. You can use this to your advantage by seeing the possibility and correct any issues.

- The bigger the picture, or the more global-wide the vision, the more variables there are to affect the outcome (humans' free will choices and actions).

- You have the ability to direct the outcome of YOUR world, by what you focus on.

Clairvoyance and Remote Viewing – Present Sight

Being able to see things in the present time without having it directly in front of you is an ability shared by many. It is also not uncommon to include other thought processes in this visual ability. You pick up clues from other sources using your intuition along with logical thought processes and memories. All of which are using your mind.

There are ways to strengthen this ability by exercising your mind.

- Solve game puzzles of all sorts, crosswords, word searches, logic, pictures, etc. Strengthen your problem-solving skills.

- Enhance your mental imagery by noticing the details around you, living mindfully.

- Take a mental walk through your home. In your mind, open drawers, cupboards, closets, and boxes. You can verify what you "see" and strengthen this ability.

- Take a mental walk through other places. Compare your memory to what it is now.

- Have a friend put something in a box. Practice mentally looking inside the box.

- When practicing a remote viewing exercise, notice what is physically catching your attention.

Retrocognition and Psychometry – Past Sight

Memory plays an important part in past visions. However, every time a memory is recalled, the mind may change the details to fill in the gaps. Some past memories go beyond the present lifetime. Many have claimed the ability to look into past life records, also called Akashic records. This cannot be denied nor confirmed. You may be able to recall your own past, and you may be able to look into the past of others.

You may get a past vision when your energy matches that of another time. For instance, during a traumatic incident, an exhilarating moment, or even during the throws of passion you may recall or receive a vision of a similar time. The deeper you become mindful of the moment, being your true Authentic Self, the clearer the vision may be. In some cases, your mind will interpret it to be in the now with all of your physical senses registering the details, making it incredibly realistic for you.

With *psychometry*, visions may come through an object. You may feel specific emotions when touching an object, traces of energy that remain. You may also receive a visual history of the object. This can also be done with photos; connecting with the object in the photo as if it is directly in front of you. Psychometry greatly overlaps with empathy. The object has taken on the energy of its surroundings and owners that you pick up on. You can pick up on such energy in rooms as well, energetic imprints, remnants of the history.

Connecting with or remembering part of the past has been helpful for some and harmful for others. Some say recalling a past memory is useful to understand issues in your current life. It is important to understand, these issues cannot be magically erased. The only way to clear your past is to learn your lessons, work through your emotions, and rebuild yourself in the present.

Some things are meant to be forgotten. You will remember what you are supposed to remember, and at the time you need to recall it. Truthfully, there is rarely a way to confirm a past vision from another time. The vision will come to you when you need to understand something or learn a lesson.

Life lessons only repeat until you learn how to change the outcome. With every new understanding, you expand your wisdom and have the opportunity to create a new way. Trust your instincts if you choose to delve into your own past. Allow it to develop naturally. If you are interested in enhancing this ability, exercise your imagination and your ability to see images in your mind.

Physically Seeing Auras and Energy Fields

Have you ever noticed a layer of color around a person, plant, animal, or object? That would be the energy field emitting from them; and yes, even objects can have an *aura* or an energy imprint.

The different colors will reflect different states of emotion and reflect the state of health. To say that a person's aura is a specific color is only reflecting what their mood is at that time. Aura colors can change as emotions and health change.

If you are able to look at a person and see this layer of color or even a slight distortion in the air surrounding the person, then you are able to physically see their energy. If you are seeing a specific color no matter where you look, it is quite possible you are seeing your own aura. Some people have been able to close their eyes and see the color of their own aura through their eyelids.

To practice seeing auras:

- Have a friend stand in front of a white wall. Allow your eyes to gaze softly on the space around them, extending from their body.

- You can also try this technique with treetops against a clear sky by softly gazing at the area around the tree. You may see a slight distortion in the air around the subject or you may see some color.

- Experiment with different lighting. Some are able to see auras or energy fields with natural light, while others can see it under luminescent lighting.

- Experiment with putting your palm facing a friend's palm, but not touching. Observe the space between the hands, moving closer and backing away. You may even feel a little tingle as the energy fields merge.

Practice

As you begin to practice these techniques, you will not readily be understood by others. In fact, many people will doubt your abilities. You may even think that once you first start getting visions, it isn't "good" or "bad" that you are getting visions. The idea here is that it is neither good nor bad. It is simply something that once you see you have an ability, to practice enhancing that ability.

Keep practicing. It also helps you to develop your Conscious Abilities if you get around people that are already practiced in this, and also those that have already developed their insight. You will find that the better support you get from others, the more your confidence grows.

Remember at first it may seem like your just imagining things, but the more you are aware of yourself in your practice, the more you fine-tune your skills. Like any muscle, you have to give it practice workouts to build up your strength

You may find pieces to life's puzzle in many places, but it is within you where the picture becomes clear.

Chapter 18: This Message is Brought to You By...???

We are deeply disturbed by how many people have fallen prey to *channelled* messages. Any *channelled* message that does not empower you to take ownership of your own life / thoughts is a false message. And this does not necessarily mean messages that have been perceived to be channelled by a spirit or alien being.

We are talking about ALL messages and quotes, throughout history that has supposedly given its followers something to look forward to. Honestly, do you really believe you are here to just be a pawn? Is your soul purpose to follow along with everything, not think, and be a sheep? Or do you have Free Will and here to learn the value of the human experience and take ownership of your own thoughts, choices, and actions?

Imagine a world where each human being was being original, true to their authentic self. Imagine a world where people are empowered and operating from a place of higher self and positivity, a higher vibrational energy frequency that uplifts not only themselves but everyone else they come in contact with

Organized religions of all times and in all regions have been guilty of *following channelled messages* since... forever. Before you discredit this, consider the concept. Ancient societies did not understand the world the way we do now. Religions were "invented" to explain what could not be explained and to manage the people. Fear-based beliefs are or were an easy way to get people to submit

The rise of "New Age" philosophies forced those who attempted to manage the general population to come up with a new way to control the masses. The ideas of aliens, the Illuminati and conspiracy theories provided the opening. The term, "Conspiracy Theory," was created by the FBI to discredit anyone who chose to research, use logic, and think for themselves. To make other believe they were "crazy" and not believe what they found in their research. It is not a theory if it is true.

When you are researching any of these ideas and beliefs, ask yourself these 3 questions. "Is this teaching coming from a place of fear?" "Or is this teaching coming from a place of love?" "How much of this message is coming from the ego?"

Most commonly used is a mind-numbing trance tactic. Whether it is through videos or in person, your physical senses are enticed. The sight sense is mesmerized with pretty pictures of scenery, graphic art, stained glass windows, laser lights, bright colors, etc. The sound sense is stimulated with harmonic music or any music. In-person, especially in group settings, music may include singing along. Singing together works by getting everyone in sync with each other.

In-person, other physical senses may be put into play. Fragrances stimulate the olfactory (smell) sense; scented candles, incense, and perfumes have been used. The touch sense is simple with soft materials, comfortable seating, books, or leaflets. The taste sensation is the least used but not unknown. Receptions often have small finger food selections; communion, and parties are some examples.

These tactics are used to get you all cozy and comfortable, feeling calm and ready to listen and absorb anything that is said. We are not saying that every message is wrong. What we are saying is: *If the message is repeatedly using negative action words, the message is false. Even by using the word <u>not</u>, these are negative words and programs the mind to consider these fear-based ideas.*

"In the future, when you read a message that tells you that there is no need to take action, no need to delve deeper into accessing and embodying your true self, that your inner work is done and you only have to wait for blessings to be bestowed upon you from an outside, higher authority, my hope is that you will not choose to believe this type of disempowering manipulation.

I hope that you will instead reclaim all energy that you had previously put into those false, yet somewhat comforting belief systems and instead choose the path of the Initiate, recognizing that YOUR truth comes from deep inside of you where your Higher Self resides. I hope that you will disengage from false prophets who try to convince you that you need to be aligned with an external group in order to ascend to the next level." (Cameron Day - http://www.ascensionhelp.com/blog/2011/09/22/discernment-lessons-channels/*

Channelling and Automatic Writing

Messages come in many forms, as mentioned in Chapter 8. One way to receive a message is through yourself; the words just come and flow out of you. There are those who claim to be channelling a message from a deceased person, extra-terrestrial beings, and some claim a deity being. Many people find comfort when an identity is attached to the message. It comes from the collective universal knowledge we are all connected to and not necessarily from a specific entity; what really matters is the message itself.

How do you become the conduit to receive a channelled message?

Just start writing (or typing). Clear your mind, center yourself, and allow the pen to glide across the paper or allow your fingers to fly across the keyboard.

If you choose to channel audibly, video yourself. Clear your mind, center yourself, and begin to speak.

You can have a general idea of what topic to begin with or you can simply do a free-write and see what flows out.

Somewhere deep within you, you already know the words. If you search for them, you might find them. But if you just let it flow out of you, the words will come.

You may surprise yourself when you go back and read (or listen to) what you wrote or said.

If it *encourages you to tap into your own innate inner power, provides a positive and thought-provoking outlook and / or stimulates you to take action with the intent of love, then it is a good* message. If it does not, let it go and move on.

Trusting the messages from the highest vibration (love), gives you the clarity that you seek. Trusting the clear messages, moving towards the highest energy vibration, you will turn on your intuition and you will have a feeling of empowerment, confirmation, hope, and having true inner confidence on your path.

Higher Self v Ego

The messages from your higher self will sound and feel a lot different than when it comes from ego. The ego wants to win, it wants to be right, and it wants to compete. You can also feel this sense when you get messages from the ego. It is a certain feeling of 'not being enough' or the feeling of 'having to prove your worth.' When you feel these things, it is usually your ego. When you get messages from your higher self it feels whole. You feel more whole and already feeling like who you are what you are seeking. There is a core frequency of love at the foundation of the vibration. Higher self includes the oneness of every human being, collective consciousness, and collective knowing. It feels less judgemental and more loving.

Chapter 19: Fate v Destiny

Fate is a result of your free will choices. You make your own fate, through what you are attracting back to you. What you are destined to do in this human life is seeded at the core of your being. Sometimes, even those poor free-will choices or you may have made in the past are very much part of your divine purpose.

If you never made poor choices or mistakes in life, how would you ever learn from them? The choices you made in the past are an accumulation of where you are now. That is why it is so key to learn from your past errors so that you can grow and evolve and make more favorable free will choices, that bring you to your destiny.

The key here is that you can only make choices based on what you know at that time. People can help guide you with your choices and have a big influence on your choices, but ultimately it is your own free will that determines your fate.

Divine Will v Free Will

"You mentioned in previous chapters about free will and how we can decide to do whatever we want in this life? What is the purpose of divine will?"

What if all the choices you made through free will, was already part of your divine will? What if there is no difference between what your free will is and what divine will is?

Divine will and free will are actually interconnected. You will make choices in your life based on what you want and prefer because you have free will. However, what if we told you that even those free will actions still led to divine will because divine will is already perfection. Divine will is already unconditional love. And Divine Will is already 'oneness' at the core of your being, the Authentic Self. Perhaps, all the choices you have made already in your life through your own free will actually serve a purpose towards a greater purpose that is part of divine will.

Your Passions

Your passions are connected to your fate. As you live authentically, following your passions you will inadvertently discover your destiny. What you love to do, along with your talents and abilities, becomes a destined passion, your purpose.

A person's fate could be anything that helps humanity. Collectively, every human is one thread in the fabric of humanity's story. No one gets anywhere without some sort of assistance from others. Whether it be through mentoring, emotional support, or physical help; humans need other humans to grow.

Balance

"Why are some people more talented in some areas and some less talented in those same areas?"

If everyone were the same, there would be no point in trying to be better at anything. Everyone has their purpose. The strengths of some humans balance the weaknesses in others. Competition can be good, pushing each other to bring out the best of our abilities. This balance allows humans to grow, advance, and evolve.

Let us use a simple example: Maybe you believe your destiny is really to be a world-renowned famous musician, you will eventually become it. As a child, you practiced all day long on your craft and were told by many people you have an incredibly special gift as a musician. You love creating music and it is something you know in your heart you were always meant to do your whole life.

The work you put into your craft every day, mixed in with your superior musical talent, and a stroke of good luck, along with extremely good timing...You are well on your way of achieving that dream of being famous worldwide as a musician.

However, if becoming a famous musician is not something you are exceptionally talented at, through divine will you can be steered in a direction and open up opportunities for you that you are more naturally talented with. You may dream of one day becoming a world-renowned musician however your talent is not at that level that a small percentage of world-renowned musicians reach. You find along the journey many exciting new things about your life because you started to venture off into careers that were more suited for you, that you excelled at, outside of music. You are content and happy that you are now living your true destiny.

This is not to discourage you at all from your dream, it is just that there is a balance in the world. The world has great musicians, artists, engineers, doctors, entrepreneurs, etc. The reason for this is because if everyone was really great at the same thing, there would be no balance in the world.

Choose your fate, based on what you are naturally talented at, and you will be fulfilled knowing you are living your best life and being true to your authentic self.

Judgment

"Judgmentalism I think is most often what happens when the desire to improve oneself exists without self-awareness." (Anonymous)

What you judge in others is something you recognize within yourself. We judge based on our own wisdom, beliefs, and Self-reflection. You cannot identify a behavior, trait, or characteristic in someone unless you have or have had similar experiences.

By going back to your Authenticity, you increase your self-awareness; and the less you feel the need to cast judgment on others. Because you know, you are still working on improving yourself.

"We are not defined by what we do, but by who we become as a result of our actions; and the things we do often become a part of who we consider ourselves to be as a result of the knowledge and wisdom we gain from our experiences." (Anonymous)

Letting Go

If you are not clear on your destiny and what you were meant to do on this planet. There is one suggestion for you. Let it go. Let go of what you think you should be doing or should be having by now. Let go of what society or outside forces have tried to lead you to believe as true. Let it all go, surrender your ego completely.

There is power in letting go. We have discussed a lot of the Conscious Abilities that you can attain throughout this book. It is true, what you think you bring about. You can also feel others' energy and also channel from your higher self. It is key to have a strong clear intention for manifesting what you want in life using free will.

The final part that is of vast importance, however, is learning the power of letting go. If you must give it an identity, think of it as surrendering to the universe. It may come as no surprise that the best manifestors and the happiest people understand and practice this balance of letting go on a regular basis.

Let go of who you think you are, what you think you're supposed to do here on earth. And simply just BE. There is a power in surrendering the divine will. When it is all said and done, your perfect flow and your perfect attainment of flow state are when knowing it is time to simply let go. Release to the universe your affirmations, beliefs, and visions and simply enjoy your life. Go about your life and feel the freedom of no thought (forget about HOW your intentions manifest) And simply being one with all that is.

Allowing yourself to completely surrender and letting go brings to you a certain joy in your spirit and a sense of liberation, a freedom that can only be accessed when you completely surrender to the universal power.

Think about the energy flow of surrendering as a way of measuring your trust in the universal power. A measure of your trust in the process / optimism. You have done the work setting your intention now watch how it all unfolds. This is also where you start to see the signs and synchronicities show up in your reality when you have let go and fully trust in the process. Come to the place in your life where you completely surrender and see the miracles of life unfold right before your eyes.

By letting it all go, your ideas of what you think you should be doing or should have by this point in your life. You are much closer in that surrender to actually coming closer to your true authentic self and thus re-aligning back to your true fate in this lifetime.

The Natural Flow

When you trust the timing of the divine flow, there is no need to force anything. When you are truly in the natural flow of your actions aligned with your authentic self you can start to move in a direction in your life that is one with the natural flow.

Trusting the natural flow of your life does not mean to do nothing. It simply means to take action from a place of inspiration. Allow yourself to be guided, not by ego...but be guided by your passion. Your internal guidance system will continue to bring you back to this wisdom and back into a deeper sense of inspirational passion.

Going back to the essence of who you truly are, trusting and being true to your authentic self, you will find a very empowering sense of inspiration that does not come from anything outside of yourself. It comes from an inner knowing that you are meant to do great things in the world, and only you can know what that is. Trusting the natural flow of your life is trusting your authentic true self.

Chapter 20: Ego

The ego is the part of consciousness that identifies the self. It is a person's sense of self-esteem, and the need to feel important. Ego is the part of consciousness that operates with fear and defensiveness. Some spiritual teachers may have you believe the ego is toxic. It can be if you allow fear to rule over your Free Will choices. Even calling yourself a "spiritual teacher" is ego because it is an identification of what you are in the physical world.

Too much ego, however, can at times be destructive. Too much ego can lead to feelings of superiority that are not necessarily healthy for day-to-day relatability with other humans. On the flip side, *humility* serves a good purpose because it allows you to connect with your inner soul essence without the need for recognition, yet with too much humility, no one may even notice you are "there."

The great news is, you have the Conscious Ability to bring yourself back to the Authentic Self and allow love to guide you. The ego's purpose is to protect oneself, a kind of an important role.

The key here is to have an equal balance between your egoic self and your soul. There are some people that have too much ego, and some that do not have enough. Some have too much humility and not enough self-esteem. You want to know what works for you, by being humble and simultaneously also having a healthy (ego) self-esteem.

Healthy Self Esteem

What is the difference between healthy self-esteem and being egotistical? Healthy self-esteem has a lot more to do with being confident in your abilities, with a desire to improve, and also being open-minded to new ideas and ways of doing things.

Being egotistical is thinking you are always "right," that you are never "wrong" and inflexible to change. Healthy self-esteem is basically knowing you are gifted at certain things, and not so gifted and others and for the most part, being happy and content with the natural direction of your life. Being proud of your past achievements, and secure with your abilities. It also means open-minded to changes along the way. There is a more natural flow to your vibration that is approachable to others when your self-esteem is healthy.

On the flip side, low self-esteem, on the other hand, is when you are constantly feeling like you cannot do something, or you do not even try something new because you are already thinking negatively about the situation. Low self-esteem can manifest in many different ways.

Such as always playing the victim in your life, or constantly blaming others for your feelings of unworthiness and lack of achievements in life. Low self-esteem also is integrated into the law of attraction. If you think poorly of yourself, you will attract events, people, and circumstances that are aligned with that low vibrational thinking.

Imagine starting the day by choosing higher vibrational thoughts. Ending the day with gratitude for the good that you did experience that day. Imagine thinking of your life as a movie, and in this movie, you play the role of someone with healthy self-esteem. You play this role, instead of life happening to you, you are consciously creating the life you truly want. By playing this role more actively, and living intentionally, you start to see that the world opens up for you in a more positive way. This is because you are now creating your reality the way you prefer it to be.

The truth each day, you are choosing either to be a victim to what life gives you, or you are choosing to be a victor. Choose healthy self-esteem by practicing a lot of the tools and applications we have already shared in this book. As you practice tuning into your authentic self, you will also find that you are developing more healthy self-esteem.

You then begin to activate - through the law of attraction healthier, more vibrant, and happier experiences in your reality. Your achievements begin to soar, and you start to have a much better appreciation for the gift of life itself.

Self-Care

As you go about your daily life, acting with kindness and compassion for others, it is important to remember to care for yourself. On an airplane, if the breathing masks were to drop you are advised to put your own mask on first before helping someone else with theirs. You must be able to continue breathing when you give yourself to the service of others. In life, you will be able to help others more when you consider your own wellbeing as well. It is absolutely ok and necessary, to stop putting everyone else first. Remember to take some time to do what is best for your own mental, emotional, and physical well-being.

We get it. You have responsibilities. You probably have a family, a home, and a job or more that takes up much of your time. Your life may very well be a constant struggle. A lot of this is because your parents did not teach you about how to be abundant and you have a hard life because your parents' beliefs about scarcity were more real than abundance. What you think, you attract. What you were taught early on as a child about life is what you grow up believing and seeing more in your current adult reality. The truth is abundance, is all there really is in life. Take a look at the trees and look at nature. It is abundant. It never stops growing there is more than enough. Look at the air you breathe, there is an abundance of it.

Were you taught as a child to love yourself? To know that there is always more than enough? Many people were conditioned early on as children not to love themselves and taught that there is always not enough. That they were not enough. Most people were raised to believe that they do not deserve the best in life. Yet, abundance is your natural state. Being happy internally is your natural state. You are enough.

Taking care of yourself and doing good for yourself is what you already are. So why do people tend to skip self-care routines? Programming. Most people were programmed subconsciously by well-meaning parents and well-meaning teachers that entered your subconscious mind to tell you the lie that you are not worthy of having a good life. Meaning, you may have been taught by example to scrimp, horde, conserve, and settle.

Indulge on occasion. Have the courage to try new experiences. Stroke the ego with these acts of self-care and believe you deserve more.

As you start to practice self-care you start to understand yourself a lot more. You start to carry yourself in a positive manner because you know you deserve the best in life, and you start to do self-care routines that benefit your overall health. It is key to be gentle at first with your self-care. Go easy with yourself at first.

Self-care is a necessity and can be seamlessly melded into your daily tasks. Sometimes, you may have to make a difficult emotional decision. Because you know overall, peace to your soul is your long-term goal.

How do you meld self-care into your daily routines? Imagine you wake up, your alarm is going off, your kids are up, the animals need to be fed... Take a moment to sit on the edge of your bed (or on the toilet) and focus on your breath. Consciously ground and center yourself. Tell yourself, "I got this." Acknowledge your heart's electromagnetic energy field; your shield and filter, clear it, thicken it, pull it close or push it out, your choice.

Take On the day! Remember, attitude is your projection and perspective. *Mindfully* work your way through your tasks. By being aware of the details, you connect with your innermost self, the Authentic Self.

If it feels wrong, <u>walk</u> <u>away</u> from it. We may often find ourselves in a situation that just does not "feel" right. Trust your gut instinct. Listen to your intuition. You can succumb to peer pressure or you can be Authentic (remember Free Will) and choose to walk away.

Say exactly what you mean. Language is a funny thing; words can often be twisted. The heart energy attached will define the energy you attract back to you.

Speak good to yourself. Many humans have an inner monologue, (surprise, not everyone has one), a conversation with themselves. If you do, be kind to yourself. *Forgive yourself* for any mistakes you make, self-reflect, learn and grow your wisdom.

Have the courage to say, "No." How many times have you done something that you really did not want to do, but you did anyway because you were too afraid to say, "No?" True, there are some situations where it may not really be an option, but for all the times you could have... Have the courage to speak up and say what you would prefer.

Have the courage to say, "Yes." Are you one of those people that when you are presented with choices, do you say, "I don't care. Whatever you would like?" And then complain, later, that you never do or go where you want? There you go... Again, have the courage to speak up and say what you would prefer.

Remember to put aside some time to do "*your thing.*" Meaning that *thing* you do that is all yours, your quiet moment, your enjoyment. It will be different for everyone. Some examples: Reading, Yoga, Puzzles, Music, Hiking, Painting, Fishing, Dancing, color a Coloring book, Photography, Sewing... The whole point is to do something that you enjoy in your solitude, connecting to your Authentic Soul Being in peace.

Self-care is about doing things that bring yourself back to good health. Whatever actions you feel are best to bring you to a place in your life where you are in sound health and in sound mind. These things that allow you to feel good, that are unique to you can be absolutely wonderful experiences, aligning to your authentic self. They say the best medicine is laughter, so go and laugh a bit more. This act of self-care is proving to yourself that you are taking good care of yourself; mentally, emotionally, and physically.

The Resource State

A simple tool to use to aid in your self-care is the clothing you wear. You most likely have work clothes, going out clothes, work-out clothes, comfortable home clothes, etc. (if you are fortunate to have such a selection - feels like a gratitude moment). Have you ever noticed the level of your attitude based on what you are wearing? Putting on a uniform allows the wearer to mentally slip into the role of the representation of said uniform. Just as changing out of your work clothes into something more *comfortable* allows you to unwind from work. The ability to detach from work is vital to your self-care. Clothing gives you a resource to guide your state of mind.

Complete the trinity with your self-care by giving attention to your physical health. (*Disclaimer: We are not doctors. If you are in need of medical attention, please, go to your doctor). Listen to your body, it knows what it needs. Eat when you are hungry. Rest when you need rest. If you do not take the time to care for yourself, your body will decide for you. Injuries and illnesses are ways for your body to make you slow down and take a break. The key to nearly anything in life is *balance and moderation*. Maintain physical health with exercise, which (remember) also, raises your vibrations.

"But I just do not have the energy to exercise." Excuses. Excuses... Are you aware that when you actually get up and move around more, you stir up a stagnant system and revitalize the system? Meaning, the more exercise you give your body, the more energy you will have. You will also more than likely be able to rest more soundly with better sleep sessions, with more exercise.\

Sleep and Insomnia

We all understand the importance of sleep and rest. But for many, sleep is elusive. If Insomnia is your nightly sleep-over friend or if you struggle with falling asleep, there are many expert opinions and solutions available. We will give you a couple of simple meditation techniques for you to try, see if you have a better rest.

Color Breathing:

As you lay down for slumber, focus on your breath. Long, slow breathing. As you inhale imagine the color blue. Imagine a clear blue sky, the blue ocean, anything that is blue and brings you calming sensations. Breathing in blue is inviting cool, calming, and relaxing to your mind. As you exhale, imagine the color orange, the bright sun, etc. Exhaling orange is releasing the activity, the creativity, thus allowing your mind to quiet down and fall asleep. Color breathing works for some.

Disconnect the Cord:

Science has proven that humans absorb energy from others. For everyone you have ever interacted with and those you interact with daily, there is some form of energetic connection. Over a lifetime, that is a lot of energy you have absorbed. Is it a wonder why some people struggle to fall asleep? Get comfortable, prepare for sleep. Think of the people you interacted with over the day. Imagine an energy cord connecting you to them, like a fiber optic cord. Now, disconnect from that person. Do not despair. You can reconnect with them after your sleep. You are never completely disconnected from your soulmates, because of quantum entanglement.

By consciously disconnecting from the people, you have interacted with, you are freeing up your energy field and bringing peace to your core. The first time you try this, you have to go back, way back to your childhood and disconnect with all of those people, through your years. You can do this in groups, i.e., your school(s), communities, cities, etc. Simply imagine all of those energy cords being released from you. It gives a whole new meaning to, "unplugging." If you fall asleep before you finish, congratulations! Mission accomplished.

Both of these suggested sleep meditations are simply a conscious way to silence your mind to allow you to drift off to sleep to get the rest you need to maintain your health.

By taking care of yourself you are also using the law of attraction to bring more of that experience that you prefer into your life. The more good things you do for yourself, the more it expands and the more good experiences you will have in your reality.

A Healthy Self Esteem and Having Your Best Life is Ahead of You.

Is your best life ahead of you? You may think that it is, and you may actually start to move in that direction based on the actions you take in the here and now. The reality is that it is your choice. If you choose to live from healthy self-esteem, learn how to move in the direction of your authentic self. Practice kindness and start doing what you know is right for your soul on a regular basis, then you are training your energy vibration to have your best life now.

Indeed, the future looks bright when you come from your authentic self. Not only will you be living your best life now, but your best life looks very promising in the future as well. As you start moving in this direction of positivity, it becomes part of your personality.

It is no longer something you have to "try to do," it becomes who you are. It becomes part of your DNA and the legacy you leave behind is something that makes a real difference in the world.

The best life you can ask for is ahead of you because you are already the best version of you in the here and now. This best life you can start living really begins and ends with understanding the power of your authentic self.

The Power of Your Authentic Self

Your authentic self is when you start to awaken to your best life. The balance between healthy self-esteem and knowing who you are is key to awakening the best life you can ever imagine. Take a look at all the people in life that have steered off course in their life. The life they lead now has no purpose, and life has become meaningless.

What happened? Was it because of outside events that controlled their mind, and thus controlled their behaviours? What really happens when a person loses touch with the meaning of their life?

What happens is that the person chose to step so far outside of who they are, that they lost touch with their purpose in life. This happens very gradually, and almost unconsciously because most people are not constantly willing to improve themselves. A lot of the techniques and tools in this book will help with your Conscious Abilities to become more magnified. It does take the actual action, doing the work however to make that a reality. It takes being willing to be courageous enough to step into that power that is your authentic self.

This does mean saying no to activities and people that no longer serve your truth and your true purpose on earth. This is not easy for a lot of people, because most are used to living their lives on autopilot. They get up, go to work, go home and watch t.v. or peruse through social media. They allow the t.v. or social media to feed their subconscious brain with negativity and go to sleep programmed to do the same thing again and call it a day and live for the weekends.

To follow trends and allow social media to dictate how you should live, is not honoring your authentic self. To silence the mind. To listen to that still inner voice, that says you are meant for greatness. That you are destined to truly make a difference in others' lives. That is an awakened soul, making moves to enhance the world. To leave the world a better place than it was before they first got here.

Life is more than that! Life can be a truly rewarding experience if one chooses to tune more to their authentic self and become the best version of who they know they could be. Being a person of light in the world, a model of positive change in the world, making their mark and making a real difference that inspires others to do the same.

To be Conscious of your Ability to make a difference in the world, in the lives of others. That is a life worth living. That is a life filled with passion and purpose.

A person that is conscious of their authentic self, to break free from patterns that no longer serve them, and move into a life that truly is one worth living; one that has a deeper meaning and a purpose to serve humanity.

Acknowledging the ego while remaining humble, gives you the Conscious Ability to develop your uniqueness, and your purpose.

Chapter 21: The Beginning of a New Era

"Human beings are not the strongest species on the planet. We're not the fastest, or maybe even the smartest. The one advantage we have is our ability to cooperate, to help each other out. We recognize ourselves in each other and were programmed for compassion, for heroism, for love, and those things make us stronger, faster and smarter. That's why we've survived. It's why we want to." (David Mazouz as Jake Bohm - t.v. 'Touch' 2012, Tim Kring)

The Meaning of Life

It is so obvious. We have been living and studying it, for all of humanity's existence. <u>Manage your heart, your emotions.</u>

How is this obviously the Meaning of Life?

Each human is born a baby. You are born innocent and full of love. As you grow, the real-world stimuli teaches you fear, and childhood can be an emotional rollercoaster. Just when you begin to get a handle on what you are feeling and experiencing... BAM! Puberty sends you on another emotional ride... Then there is adulting. Years of discovering yourself, managing your life with new experiences and growing your wisdom, and *mid-life crisis* takes its toll... And least not forget the seniors, dealing with menopause, fluctuating / decreasing hormones, and senility. It is all as if we humans are designed to break, self-heal, and grow by finding and growing the love within us, managing our hearts.

Now imagine how much smoother we can make these emotional rollercoaster rides at these pivotal points of a person's life; understanding that humans can absorb energy from others. With this knowledge, we have the Conscious Abilities to guide, and by example, mentor the next generations to being authentic with a healthy state of mind, managing and owning what they feel, taking personal accountability for their choices, all leading to and by love… Imagine that. Make it so.

Human beings have thrived on earth for centuries. We have faced many challenges in the span of our history. The humans' ability to adapt is how we continue. Helping our fellow humans, through kindness and compassion, keeps the human race alive.

"Seven billion people on a tiny planet, suspended in the vastness of space all alone. How we make sense of that is the great mystery of our frail existence. Maybe it's being alone in the universe that holds us all together, keeps us needing one another in the smallest of ways, creating a quantum entanglement of you, of me, of us. And if that's really true, then we live in a world where anything is possible." (David Mazouz as Jake Bohm - t.v. 'Touch' 2012, Tim Kring)

The New Era and Real News

There is a lot of conspiracy out there about what is real news and what is fake news. The truth will come when people are tuned into a higher level of consciousness. This means that being true to one's authentic self and seeing the world clearly can end fake news and be more informed with what is true and righteous.

You see, people in power want to remain in power. Fear tactics are used to keep the general population under control and believing we need these people in charge. (This is also referred to as "fear-mongering"). Religions were created for this very reason. The mainstream media / news is manipulated to grow our fear so that we continue to "trust" those in charge. But they are the ones creating the fear. *Who is really in charge*? YOU ARE. Free Will determines this fact. The reason for the use of fearmongering is for one reason, and one reason only. That reason is control. If they can keep you in fear, they are using that energy and panic that you are emanating, to control your way of life.

The good news is that we are entering a new era. The more real news is coming into mainstream media news channels. This is because more people are tuning into the truth within themselves. People's lie-detectors are increasing in frequency and can intuitively see if something is coming from a place of truth or not. Those who can see beyond social conditioning and indoctrination, have the ability to discern truth from deception, and are able to recognize when their heart speaks louder than any voice.

As people tune in to the new era, they are tuned in to what is real and not false. They can then come from a place of greater confidence in speaking the truth and with the confidence into being truly themselves. When one steps into the power of the authentic self, they speak and act with a confidence that is pure, driven by love.

This allows others to have the courage to research and come together with real news. And in this shared truth, humanity moves forward. This is what moves the human race forward. To fully be in the light and know that what is true, will always be true and to help assist those that are further behind. To inspire others to seek the truth and encourage others to do the same.

To move in this direction, will take compassion, and understanding of people's levels of consciousness and understanding. With patience, we will see that humanity is indeed moving forward, and those that do evil will continue to suffer. Those that continue to do good in the world will thrive, in an era that leads to an unbelievably beautiful life, a beautiful life being one with the authentic self and one that is righteous, honest, and pure.

Faith

To have complete trust or confidence in someone or something, a person, thing, or concept. Faith is not a religious term. It is the very act of having confidence in something, genuinely believing.

It does not matter if your faith or belief is in a deity, a talisman, a crystal, a stone, or even a lucky coin. The real power is in the belief. It is that absolute belief the mind directs to the external is what makes it real. A thought sparks the energy; and when it is matched with heartfelt emotions, the energy force is magnified.

Have faith that the human race is moving towards a greater understanding of the collective consciousness. Have faith that we, as humans, can Be Authentic. Have faith in humanity and Be the example. Know and believe this to be true, and it will be true. Have faith, we can make a better world. It begins with You.

We are all connected at the highest conscious level; like one big brain. When you consciously make an effort, thoughtfully, emotionally, and physically to be an example of love, kindness, and compassion; then we have the ability to shift this world out of fear and into a love state. No more dividing the people. No more labels, other than your name. No more judgment. No more fear... Just LOVE.

Equality does not mean equal outcome. Everyone has different strengths. Equality means we all have an equal opportunity to bring out our strengths. When we work together through love, our strengths will balance with the weakness in others. Together we are able to adapt, advance, and evolve.

Rebuild

Regardless of whatever stage you are in life, you can always come back to your authentic trinity being. This is the intent of the book. It matters not what happens in the outside world and has everything to do with what is going on in your inner world. If your inner world is good, the outside world follows what is already within you. If you are reading this book, you have either survived the threat of humanity's mass extinction or you are a product of those who survived. This is your opportunity to rebuild a world with love. Learn from the mistakes and wisdom of your ancestors. Discover your authentic self and make your reality something we can all be proud to say, "We did it! We Are One."

We leave you with your Free Will choice, to accept your choices by taking personal accountability for your actions, accepting responsibility for your creations. We ask that you be a part of bridging the gap between the spiritual realm and the physical realm, and to guide the generations to follow, with love through kindness and compassion. Uniting all of humanity.

Completion and Intuition

What if the completion of life is what you always felt it to be? The meaning of life is what you always felt and intuitively knew it to be and consist of? That completing this life meant you believed in your intuition enough to know what the meaning of life really meant. When your life is all said and done, did you live the life that you intuitively knew to be true for you? That you can say you did your best while you lived here on earth, to live your truth?

Not the truth that comes from the ego, but what your soul always felt to be true? Are you that authentic? What if completing this life was led by your soul and what your heart knew to be true? The truth is, what you already know to be true, is within you. You just have to bring it out into this world.

It is our intent that this book has served you well and given you the techniques to use your conscious ability by aligning with your authentic self and completing your life cycle.

Coming full circle if you will. To a place that you always have known yourself to be, which quite naturally is the perfection of love and with the intent to live this life to the best of your abilities, leaving this world a much better place because you existed here.

You think, so you Live. Your spirit is alive and expressed through your heart. Live with expressions of Love. What is Love? *Love is the unselfish loyal and benevolent concern for the good of another, expressed through kindness and compassion.* You have a body, use it to laugh and enjoy being alive. Live fiercely. Love passionately. Laugh frequently.

Live. Love. Laugh. Be Authentic.

Chapter 22: Dear Human,

This book has become the completion of the thoughts and wisdom I always knew about, which can further help you on your journey in this physical life. Before this book was written, I already had a vision that it would inspire and empower the lives of millions upon millions of people across the globe.

Before a single word was written for this book, I already knew it would reach your heart, dear reader. Long before the words were written in this book, I was completely certain and knew without a shadow of a doubt, that the words expressed in this book were not just words, but a transfer of pure loving energy from my soul to yours. I believe this book would in some form act as a guiding light for you on your journey.

It is my intent that you are inspired and use the tools here and ideas as a road map to better the quality of your life experience while on earth, and thus making a positive difference in the world as well.

Every step on your journey will require you to, and give you the opportunity to, step back into your authentic self and understand the power within you to transform your life, and to also help inspire and transform the lives of others. Use the wisdom shared in this book to further develop your life, connecting you back to the Authentic Self and making this world a better place.

With Love,
Baker Jacinto

Authors Biography:

Baker Jacinto, also known simply as *Baker*, was born in Baguio, Philippines. As an infant at 6 months old his parents brought him to America. He graduated from college in Cal-State San Bernardino, with a major in business administration-real estate concentration. He was raised all of his life in the United States and is a philosopher, mystic, poet, and law of attraction expert. And a passionate author.

He has lived in both California and Arizona where he was trained in rhetoric, mystical, new age thought, and both western and eastern philosophy. He enjoys traveling the world, exercise, and meditation. He currently is a landlord living peacefully and happily in the Philippines and lives a healthy, blessed, and balanced lifestyle.

Deidra Rae is an American, born in Southern California, U.S.A. Generation X. She earned the nickname, "Mama," after spending months in public forums, guiding and encouraging others. Rather than pointing people on a set path like many "spiritual guides," she prefers to support others in finding their own way much like a mother with her children.

Born under Sagittarius, Deidra Rae draws from her fire sign a direct and honest (sometimes brutally so) approach and eschews tact and coddling; this applies to both her criticism and encouragement. Many have, at first, found themselves offended by her straightforward manner only to find an appreciation for her once they get past the initial shock.

In her daily life, Deidra Rae teaches martial arts to local children. Holding a black belt in Kenpo Karate with influences from several other styles, she uses her teaching method (just as straightforward in person as it is online) to help her students develop not only the ability to defend themselves and others but to also manage their emotions with the confidence to excel in school and in life. Her goal, along with continuing to grow as a martial artist, is to see her students and those she guides to exceed her own abilities and go on to teach younger generations.

She loves adventure and takes on life while laughing in the face of fear. She has travelled most of the U.S. and spent a portion of her childhood as a missionary in the Philippines. She has been studying, experiencing, and gaining an understanding of the world her whole life.

She loves to learn and try new things. And she analyses everything. Her mind never stops; always taking in information and putting the pieces of the puzzle together to make sense of it all. She has studied (and continues to understand) history, human anatomy and physiology, philosophy, quantum physics, metaphysics, and organized religions.

Made in the USA
Thornton, CO
09/16/22 16:47:36